THE VIETNAM WAR

Twentieth-Century Wars
General Editor: Jeremy Black

Published titles

Forthcoming

Twentieth-Century Wars
Series Standing Order ISBN 0-333-77101-X

You can receive future titles in this series as they are published. To place a standing order please contact your bookseller or, in the case of difficulty, write to us at the address below with your name and address, the title of the series and the ISBN quoted above.

Customer Services Department, Macmillan Distribution Ltd
Houndmills, Basingstoke, Hampshire RG21 6XS, England

THE VIETNAM WAR

David L. Anderson

First published 2005 by
PALGRAVE MACMILLAN
Houndmills, Basingstoke, Hampshire RG21 6XS and
175 Fifth Avenue, New York, N.Y. 10010
Companies and representatives throughout the world

PALGRAVE MACMILLAN is the global academic imprint of
the Palgrave Macmillan division of St. Martin's Press, LLC and of
Palgrave Macmillan Ltd, Macmillan® is a registered trademark in the
United States, United Kingdom and other countries. Palgrave is a
registered trademark in the European Union and other countries.

ISBN 0–333–96337–7 paperback
ISBN 0–333–96336–9 hardback

This book is printed on paper suitable for recycling and made from
fully managed and sustained forest sources.

A catalogue record for this book is available from the British Library.

A catalog record for this book is available from the Library of Congress

10   9   8   7   6   5   4   3   2   1
14   13   12   11   10   09   08   07   06   05

Transferred to digital printing in 2007.

Contents

v

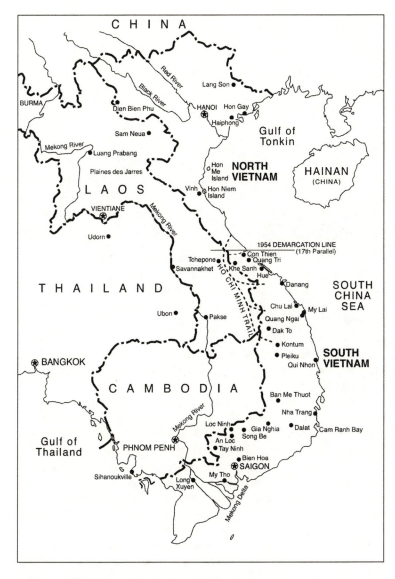

Vietnam After the 1954 Geneva Agreement

From *The U.S. Government and the Vietnam War: Executive and Legislative Roles and Relationships, Part I: 1945–1960*, United States Government Printing Office (1984).

Preface

The Vietnam War ended in 1975 with the final unification of that divided country under the sole authority of the government in Hanoi. The beginning of the war is more difficult to date with precision because the Vietnam War was, indeed, several wars, but a useful starting point for historians is the opening of hostilities between the French and Vietminh in late 1945. The Vietnam War, then, is a conflict that endured for 30 years, cost billions of dollars, and resulted in the deaths of tens of thousands of French and American soldiers and hundreds of thousands of Vietnamese. It was not a world war, but it was one of the major military conflicts of the twentieth century, and its origins, course, and outcome fundamentally affected not only Vietnam but also France, the United States, and the international community.

There has been a flood of books and articles written about the Vietnam conflict. In 1984, Richard Dean Burns and Milton Leitenberg published *The Wars of Vietnam, Cambodia, and Laos, 1945–1982: A Bibliographic Guide* (Santa Barbara, CA: ABC-Clio) that had 5000 items in it. Burns and Lester Brune did a revised and updated bibliography in 1992, *America and the Indochina Wars, 1945–1990* (Claremont, CA: Regina Books), with 3500 additional books and articles listed. In the past decade a steady outpouring of new works has added hundreds of additional titles. Much of this publishing phenomenon derives from the continuing controversy that surrounds the reasons for, and results of, the war and from a kind of morbid fascination with what went wrong. This book will explore the nature of the debate over the war while also seeking to provide a clear narrative account of the historical events.

Although this study discusses the French colonial war from 1945 to 1954 and the final Vietnamese phase of the conflict from 1973 to 1975, the primary focus is on the American war in Vietnam. It was the Americanization of the war that caused it to go on for so long and to reach such massive proportions with over a half-million US troops in Vietnam by 1968. This American military intervention, the longest overseas deployment of US troops in combat in American history, came to embroil domestic American society in protests and confrontation. The war also placed enormous strains on the Western alliance and was a significant influence on eventual US moves to lessen tensions with the Soviet Union and the People's Republic of China.

This book draws upon the many excellent works that constitute the vast literature on the war. Incorporating the best practices of these modern war studies, it is an examination of military, political, diplomatic, social, and economic issues. It adheres primarily to what historiographers term a liberal–realist critique of the US war, an approach which contends that policy makers magnified the strategic importance of Southeast Asia and underestimated the strength of the Vietnamese communist movement.

1

Causes: Colonialism and Containment

For centuries the Vietnamese people resisted domination by their power-ful Chinese neighbors and struggled to unify their country as an indepen-dent state. They ultimately freed themselves from China's claims of political authority and achieved national unity only to fall victim to French imperialism. France ruled Vietnam and the neighboring kingdoms of Laos and Cambodia as colonies from the late nineteenth century into the twen-tieth century, until the Japanese occupation of Southeast Asia during the Second World War set the stage for the Vietminh war against the French beginning in 1945. Because the charismatic leader of the Vietminh move-ment, Ho Chi Minh, was a communist closely associated with the Soviet and Chinese Communist Parties, his challenge to France was also a Cold War issue. After the Second World War the United States emerged as the powerful leader of the coalition of Western democracies opposed to any political or military expansion of communism. US policy makers did not condone French colonialism, but they believed that US global security could not allow an ally of Moscow and Beijing to be successful in Southeast Asia against France, an ally of the United States. By the end of the administration of President Harry Truman in 1953, the United States was providing much of the financing for the French War because Paris was losing the political will to continue the conflict that critics termed the 'dirty war.' Geopolitical strategy, economics, domestic US politics, and cultural arrogance shaped the growing American involvement in Vietnam.

The origins of Vietnam

Vietnam is a centuries-old nation with a proud cultural and political tradition. During the Vietnam War of the mid-twentieth century, people in the West generally thought of Vietnam as a small and underdeveloped nation. It is, in fact, not a small but an average-sized country with territory and population comparable to Spain, Egypt, or Poland. In 1960 its total population was slightly more than 30 million with about 2 million more people living in North Vietnam, that is, north of the seventeenth parallel, than in South Vietnam. Almost 90 percent of the people were ethnically Vietnamese. The principal minority was Chinese, and there were small numbers of other minorities, most notably the so-called Montagnards or mountain people of the Central Highlands. In territory, Vietnam is about 1000 miles (1600 km) in length from the northern border with China to the southern tip on the South China Sea. It is very narrow in the middle near the seventeenth parallel, about 40 miles (64 km) wide, but its width reaches almost 300 miles (480 km) in the north and 125 miles (200 km) in the south. The total land area of 126,000 square miles (328,000 square km) was almost equally divided between North and South Vietnam, and each half was approximately equivalent in size to England and Wales combined.

The Vietnamese people and culture first appeared in the valley and delta of the Red River in the north. By the middle of the twentieth century, this area, the Mekong River Delta in the south, and the narrow coastal plain along the length of the country contained most of the population. About 80 percent of Vietnam is mountains, forests, marshes, and grasslands that are sparsely populated. Throughout most of Vietnam's history, the primary economic activity on the habitable land has been rice cultivation, but fishing along the lengthy coastline and in the rivers and canals has also been a primary source of food and income. Most of the country's minimal mineral resources are in the north. As has been true throughout the world, Vietnam has experienced a major migration from rural to urban areas that began in the early 1950s and has continued ever since. The largest city is Ho Chi Minh City, which was previously called Saigon and was the capital of South Vietnam. The capital of North Vietnam and the national capital since the end of the war is Hanoi, the second largest city. Major port cities are Haiphong and Danang.

There are considerable regional variations in Vietnam that have been significant throughout its history. The long distance in Vietnam from the cradle of its culture along the Red River in the north to areas in the south and contests for possession of territory from rival peoples meant that different areas came under Vietnamese control at different times and in different ways. Variations in land elevations and in rainfall patterns also created different patterns of life. After the entire country became united, its rulers set up three roughly defined administrative regions – Bac Bo in the north, Trung Bo in the central region, and Nam Bo in the south – in an effort to make the new unity effective. When the French colonized Vietnam in the nineteenth century, however, they sought to make these divisions even more complete in order to prevent Vietnamese unity. They designated the area around Hanoi up to the Chinese border as Tonkin, the area from immediately south of the Red River Delta down through the Central Highlands as Annam, and the area around the Mekong River Delta as Cochinchina.[1]

Centuries before the French presence, however, the principal external threat and influence on the Vietnamese came from China. According to Vietnamese legend, they shared a common origin with the Chinese that dated back into the third millennium BCE, but the earliest historical record of a distinctive Vietnamese people is dated 207 BCE. It is a Chinese account of a conquest of the area around the Red River Delta and its incorporation into a kingdom referred to as Nam Viet or Nan Yue (South Yue) ruled by a Chinese general from a capital near Guangzhou in present-day China. This date marks the beginning of a thousand years of Chinese rule. In a literal sense Nam Viet was a separate kingdom from China, but it had a Chinese ruler who imposed a Chinese-style bureaucratic government and the Chinese system of rice cultivation. In 111 BCE, however, the powerful Han Dynasty, one of China's strongest ruling families, annexed Nam Viet as a province of China, and it remained a Chinese province until ADE 939.[2]

During the thousand years that the northern part of what is now Vietnam was under Chinese rule, the Vietnamese absorbed many aspects of Chinese culture. Vietnam's own culture remained strong, however, and the determination to be free of Chinese control never died. Over this same period, China incorporated many other border peoples and made them essentially Chinese. The Vietnamese retained distinctive elements of their way of living, such as chewing betel nut, practicing totemism, and sustaining a social structure that, especially unlike China, gave a high status to women. The most notable impact of Chinese culture was on the Vietnamese ruling class. The Chinese philosophy of Confucianism, in particular, created a spiritual reverence for the authority of the emperor, the so-called Mandate of Heaven, and extended that model into a social and political hierarchy. Dominant Vietnamese families embraced this concept to legitimize their authority and created, in Chinese fashion, a bureaucracy of gentry officials, or mandarins, schooled in Confucianism through which to exercise power. The vast majority of Vietnamese were peasant farmers and fishermen, however, and for them Confucianism, the more mystical concepts of Taoism,

Chinese interpretations of Buddhism, and traditional Vietnamese beliefs blended together. Because the peasants clung more tightly to Vietnamese traditions than did the mandarins, the small villages throughout the country became the strongest and most enduring symbols of Vietnamese identity. This village allegiance was an important part of Vietnamese society into the modern era.[3]

The degree of actual Chinese control over its Vietnamese province had varied considerably over the centuries, and finally in 938 a Vietnamese force won a decisive naval victory that ended Chinese claims of authority. A Vietnamese state called Dai Viet extended from Tonkin down to about Danang, but its survival and stability were far from secure. In 1076 China's Sung Dynasty tried unsuccessfully to retake Vietnam, and in the late thirteenth century the Vietnamese repulsed a Mongol invasion. In the early 1400s the mighty Ming Dynasty sent a force that reoccupied Vietnam for about two decades, but it too failed to remove the independence for which the Vietnamese had long struggled.

Even as the Vietnamese were managing to survive against serious external threats, they were engaged in internal contests for political dominance. Several strong families vied for control until the Ly family established a stable central government in the eleventh century. After about two centuries the Tran Dynasty succeeded the Ly in a peaceful transition. Stability came under both of these dynasties through their successful modeling of China's gentry bureaucracy as a means to conduct civil affairs. The survival of an independent Vietnam, however, brought friction with a powerful neighbor to the south, the Kingdom of Champa. The Vietnamese fought the Chams in a series of wars that brought an end to the Tran Dynasty and tempted the Ming to make its assault on Vietnam. In this crisis, a great hero of Vietnamese history, Le Loi, emerged.

Le Loi's defeat of the Ming invaders in 1428 forced China to recognize Vietnam's independence. He then founded the Le Dynasty and began what became known as the 'March to the South.' In 1471 the Vietnamese finally conquered Champa and absorbed its territory. Over the next two and a half centuries they proceeded to occupy lands along the coast until they had secured possession of the Mekong Delta from the Khmer Kingdom (Cambodia). By 1701 Vietnam had reached its full extent from the Chinese border in the north to the Cau Mau Peninsula in the south.[4]

As Vietnam expanded, central control became difficult to maintain. Twice during the March to the South the country divided into northern and southern kingdoms. One of these divisions was from 1540 to 1592, but the second lasted longer from 1673 to 1802. During this later period, the Trinh family ruled Tonkin, although an impotent Le Dynasty nominally remained. The Nguyen family was dominant in the south, claimed the imperial throne of Vietnam belonged to it, and was responsible for the taking of Cochinchina from the Khmers. The dividing line between the areas of Trinh and Nguyen control was at approximately the seventeenth parallel, which coincidentally would mark the boundary between North Vietnam and South Vietnam in 1954. Also, in the early 1500s the first European contact with Vietnam occurred with the appearance of Portuguese traders. By the seventeenth century, Portugal, Spain, Holland, France, and England were carrying on some trade with Vietnam. Portuguese and Spanish Jesuit priests and the French Society of Foreign Missions combined missionary efforts with commerce, but the Vietnamese grew suspicious of these religious activities and curtailed them in the late 1600s.

In 1777 three brothers from the village of Tay Son near Hue led a revolt that overthrew Nguyen rule in the south. This Tay Son Rebellion demonstrated how, throughout the years of territorial expansion, the local villages had remained not only guardians of Vietnamese culture but also centers of rebel resistance to central authority. In 1786 the Trinh in the north fell victim to this same rebellion. As fighting concentrated in Tonkin, however, a prince of the Nguyen family, Nguyen Anh, seized Cochinchina with the help of a French missionary, Pigneau de Behaine. Pigneau tried to arrange for official French assistance for Nguyen Anh in a plan that would have given France possession of the port of Tourane, which the Vietnamese called Danang. Paris rejected the scheme, but Pigneau obtained funds from French merchants to pay for mercenaries and arms for Nguyen Anh with the understanding that the Vietnamese leader would protect French missionaries. With this assistance, Nguyen Anh defeated the Tay Son brothers in 1802 and declared himself Emperor Gia Long, ruler of a united Vietnam.[5]

The Nguyen Dynasty established by Gia Long made the city of Hue the imperial capital, and this Chinese-style monarchy became Vietnam's last dynasty. The last emperor of the Nguyen line was Bao Dai, who abdicated the throne in 1945. Long before, however, French colonialism and radical nationalist resistance to colonial rule had reduced the emperor to a figurehead. Gia Long recognized that China remained a potential danger to his country and sent tribute missions, emissaries bearing generous gifts, to Beijing to ensure good relations. He also acknowledged Pigneau's help by tolerating French missionary activities.

Subsequent emperors persecuted missionaries, however. In turn, the French government became increasingly aggressive in demanding protection of the missionaries. Like other European nations at the time, France was also searching for markets and raw materials for its increasingly industrialized economy, and Vietnam seemed a good source for both. In 1858 Paris sent a large naval force to Vietnam, the first of a series of events that led by the end of the century to French colonization of Vietnam and the neighboring states of Laos and Cambodia.[6]

French colonialism

On 1 September 1858, a fleet of 14 French vessels took possession of Tourane. Although heat and disease required the occupiers to withdraw in a few months, a relentless pattern of small and large French military assaults on Vietnam had begun. In 1859 another French force took the village of Saigon in the south in the hope that the Mekong River would prove to be a commercial passageway into China. Exploration of the river found inland transit blocked by falls and rapids, but in 1862 Emperor Tu Duc agreed to transfer much of Cochinchina to France as a colony. The same year France created a protectorate over the royal government of Cambodia. Trying to gain an economic foothold in South China before British commercial interest moved out of Burma into the region, France then began efforts to possess the Red River route. A series of military clashes ensued placing French units against Vietnamese forces and also against southern Chinese armies seeking to block Western imperial expansion into their territory. In 1874 Tu Duc granted further concessions to France in Cochinchina and around Hanoi and Haiphong. Fighting that was quite heavy at times continued. Although the emperor's court remained in Hue, in 1883 after Tu Duc's death, Annam and Tonkin became French protectorates, and the Laotian monarchy, too, fell under French control in 1893. China signed a convention in 1885 recognizing French control of the area. In 1897, France formally organized what it called the Indochina Union of Cochinchina, Annam, Tonkin, Cambodia, and Laos. Administered by a governor general in Hanoi, French Indochina was, by whatever name, a fully established French colony.

France's rule over its colony was incredibly brutal and exploitative. Indeed, the colonial authorities tried to extinguish the identity of the Vietnamese within the five-part colony. The rulers referred to the people of Vietnam as Annamites. The Europeans claimed to be civilizing the local inhabitants. This *mission civilisatrice* sought to impose Western language, culture, religion, and economic structure. Despite the thin veneer of reform rhetoric, the purpose was to control the territory and resources of Indochina for the benefit of France. The Nguyen monarchy remained in Hue as an effete relic, but real and unlimited authority was in the hands of the governors general in Hanoi, who did not hesitate to imprison or execute anyone who defied their will. Although some of the old elite clung to a hope for a revival of the Confucian order, much of the gentry class was either silenced or came to collaborate with the colonial masters as a way of survival.[7]

French colonialism deprived the Vietnamese of their political independence, and it impoverished the vast majority of the Vietnamese people. Already a country of farmers and fishermen, colonial Vietnam developed no industries but became a major producer of raw materials, specifically rice, rubber, and coal. Having for centuries lived off the small plots belonging to their families or clans, many villagers lost their lands and became low-paid plantation workers, share croppers, or miners in large operations owned by French companies and absentee landlords or a small class of wealthy Vietnamese collaborators. High taxes, exorbitant rents, and fees charged by banks, moneylenders, and rice-brokers kept the majority in debt and poverty while a minority grew rich. There was virtually no middle class. Colonialism brought economic deprivation, political impotence, weakening of village autonomy, rising illiteracy, and social tension. Not surprisingly, radical anticolonial movements appeared among the Vietnamese. Revolution, not reform, seemed to many Vietnamese to be the only answer to economic exploitation, political repression, and cultural stagnation. There were reformers who looked to China and Japan for ideas of how to respond to Western imperialism while conserving traditional Asian values. In addition, radical ideas of national self-determination, revolutionary class struggle, and party dictatorship appeared in China in the 1920s that had repercussions in Vietnam. The French colonial years were an era of frustration for many Vietnamese, oppressed by the foreign intruders and a native, Francophile upper class.

With no middle class to form a constituent base and French officials quick to silence any dissent from their authority, Vietnamese patriots found it virtually impossible to form modern political parties to represent the interests of the people. Initially, the small strata of Vietnamese intellectuals who had received a traditional education in the Confucian classics had to overcome their own disdain for Western political concepts of social and political progress. By the 1890s, Japan had become a model for reformers in China and Vietnam of what became known as self-strengthening, that is, adapting Western technology and institutions to serve Asian values. In Vietnam, Phan Boi Chau and others created a Modernization Society that advocated the creation of a constitutional monarchy to revitalize the imperial court at Hue. Inspired by Sun Yat-sen's movement in China that had led to the creation of a republican government there in 1912, the Modernization Society became the Revitalization Society with the same goal for Vietnam. Chau's movement was not strong enough to break French control, and its efforts to propagandize and agitate for change eventually led to Chau's arrest in 1925 and confinement for life. Phan Boi Chau is a significant representative of an emerging search among Vietnamese for how to move beyond isolated protests of French and elite mistreatment of the masses toward some form of organized force for social change.[8]

The French authorities outlawed Vietnamese political parties, except for a token group representing the collaborationist elite, thus compelling nationalist groups opposed to French rule to organize and operate in secret. There were a number of such clandestine cells, but most of them were very small. The Vietnam Quoc Dan Dong (VNQDD) or Vietnam Nationalist Party managed, however, to mount a dramatic if futile challenge to the colonial overlords in February 1930. It had a moderate socialist program and tried to use armed rebellion to ignite a popular uprising aimed at creating a Vietnamese republic, much as the Nationalist Party or Guomindang had accomplished in China. VNQDD bands numbering from 50 to 300 attacked several French military posts and inflicted the heaviest losses, 12 French dead, at Yen Bay. No uprising ensued, and the colonial forces soon captured, imprisoned, and executed many of the rebels, although some escaped to China. French Indochina appeared firmly in the possession of the Europeans.[9]

Ho Chi Minh and Vietnamese communism

In 1930 as the French squelched the VNQDD, the party that would eventually break the power of the colonialists came secretly into existence. It was the Indochina Communist Party (ICP), and it had the leadership, discipline, and clarity of purpose – a call for national independence and social equality – to enable it to challenge effectively the wealth and power of the Europeans. The individual most responsible for the creation of the ICP was Ho Chi Minh, its charismatic leader whose humble image masked his tremendous tactical skills. Ho is often labeled the father of the Vietnamese revolution because he combined an innate understanding of Vietnamese history, a thorough grounding in Marxist–Leninist theory, and his own ardent and self-confident patriotism to create a successful national liberation movement.[10]

Ho Chi Minh was born near Vinh in northern Annam in 1890, a time when French colonial power was coming into full sway.[11] His name at birth was Nguyen Sinh Cung, and he did not take the name Ho Chi Minh until many years later. Although educated to be a mandarin, his father had lost his government post for failure to implement colonial laws. From Phan Boi Chau, a friend of his father, the young Ho undoubtedly learned some lessons about political activism. He received a good formal education at a fine school in Hue in preparation to be a teacher. Taking a job in a ship's galley, he left Vietnam in 1911 to see the world. He was in France when the First World War began, and there he joined the French Socialist Party. Using the pseudonym Nguyen Ai Quoc (Nguyen the Patriot), he appealed unsuccessfully to the negotiators at the Versailles Peace Conference to apply President Woodrow Wilson's rhetoric about self-determination to French Indochina. Like many Vietnamese, he was deeply embittered by the French rule of his country, and in the writings of Vladimir Lenin he found answers to many of his questions about colonialism. Particularly striking was Lenin's argument that, for colonial people, the struggle for independence was part of the universal class struggle of workers against the owners of capital. For a youthful Asian patriot this idea was a heady doctrine that placed blame for the plight of the Vietnamese people on an inherent weakness in Western society and made the Vietnamese struggle part of a historic pattern of heroic proportions.

In 1920 Ho became a founding member of the French Communist Party. As a political agitator he used a variety of aliases, but generally was known during the 1920s and 1930s as Nguyen Ai Quoc. In 1923 he went to Moscow and began work for the Communist International or Comintern. Working for the Comintern in south China in 1925, he created the Vietnamese Revolutionary Youth League to train young activists in Leninist doctrine and tactics. His next step was the consolidation of various secret groups into the Vietnamese Communist Party in February 1930, but his Comintern superiors in Moscow thought that name put too much attention on national independence and insisted that it be changed to Indochina Communist Party.

During the 1930s, the ICP remained small with only a few hundred members scattered throughout Southeast Asia and southern China. British colonial authorities in Hong Kong detained Nguyen Ai Quoc for some months on investigation of suspicious activities but eventually released him, and he returned to Moscow. The two major communist parties, in the Soviet Union and China, were going through their own internal leadership and doctrinal struggles during the decade, and the correct strategy for the small organization in Indochina remained to be decided. The worldwide economic depression had created worsening conditions for the peasants and workers in Vietnam, and the rise of the fascist dictatorship in Germany and the militarists in Japan had produced new political challenges for communist leaders everywhere. Within party circles, Nguyen Ai Quoc had long been an advocate of a united-front strategy in which communists would form temporary alliances with national revolutionaries and democratic socialist parties to battle reactionaries and imperialists. In 1938, after the outbreak of the Sino–Japanese War, the Comintern allowed him to return to south China to work with the Chinese Communist Party and its rival the Nationalist Party (Guomindang) in the anti-Japanese war.

Among Vietnamese revolutionaries, Nguyen Ai Quoc was a legendary and mysterious figure, even assumed to be dead by some reports. In China the Communist–Nationalist united front gave him freedom to move about and prepare for the opportunity to achieve his long-sought goal of freedom for Vietnam. He established contact with members of the ICP, including Pham Van Dong and Vo Nguyen Giap, and they decided in 1940, after the German occupation of France and the formation of the puppet government in Vichy, to create the League for the Independence of Vietnam (Viet Nam Doc Lap Dong Minh). The ICP conceived of this organization, known as the Vietminh, to be broadly inclusive of all patriotic Vietnamese who would join to defeat French colonial rule. In January 1941, for the first time in almost 30 years, Nguyen Ai Quoc slipped secretly back into Vietnam to the border village of Pac Bo traveling under the name Ho Chi Minh (He Who Enlightens). Early in 1941 Japan began to establish military bases in Indochina with the acquiescence of the colonial officials. On 10 May at Pac Bo, Ho convened the Eighth Plenum of the Indochina Communist Party, which formally established the Vietminh Front. The founding documents proclaimed its goals to be the liberation of Vietnam from French colonial rule and Japanese military occupation.[12]

The Franco–Vietminh War

The Vietminh would eventually achieve its objectives but only after the conclusion of a world war and an intense military conflict with a France determined to hold on to its colonial jewel. Ho Chi Minh and the ICP understood that the Second World War was a strategic opportunity for the cause of Vietnamese independence. The fall of France to the Nazi advance in Europe had left colonial officials in Indochina largely on their own. They struck deals with the Japanese military that allowed them to continue to collect rents and taxes in the colony in return for offering no resistance to Japan's demands for port facilities, air fields, and raw materials in Indochina. Thus they avoided the humiliating defeats suffered by British, Dutch, and American forces in Malaya, Singapore, Hong Kong, the East Indies, and the Philippines, but the French also isolated themselves and aligned their fate with continued Japanese success.

The Japanese occupation of Southeast Asia was a military and political disaster for the French and all the colonial powers. Although the Japanese invaders eventually met defeat, largely at the hands of forces from the United States, Britain, Australia, and New Zealand, the region would never again be the same. The Europeans had once claimed unquestioned authority, but now had lost face. Their right to rule had been called into question not by another European power, but by an Asian power that had claimed to be fighting the United States and Britain in defense of the principle of Asia for Asians. Tokyo intended for this propaganda to generate support for Japan, but it had also become a rallying cry for local independence movements like the Vietminh. Military operations in the region also helped break the advantage in modern weaponry that colonial forces had previously held over resistance fighters. In some cases Japanese or Western forces helped arm local fighters and in other cases, especially near the end of the war, weapons simply fell into local hands.

From its remote base along the China–Tonkin border, the Vietminh Front worked to build its strength. Although Ho renamed the river outside his headquarters 'Lenin' in honor of his personal hero, he and the ICP cadre avoided mention of social revolution when recruiting followers and talked instead of national independence and democracy. Benefiting from discontent fueled by French and Japanese actions and an outbreak of famine, the Vietminh recruited about 5000 resistance fighters, whom Vo Nguyen Giap organized into an armed brigade. The Vietminh tried to coordinate anti-Japanese activity in south China with American intelligence officers from the Office of Strategic Services (OSS), but it was too little known to attract much attention. In 1945, however, with the war almost over, Ho did meet with members of the OSS Deer Team, who were struck by his leadership qualities.[13]

At the end of the Japanese war the opportunity for which the Vietminh had been preparing presented itself. Allied forces had liberated France from Nazi occupation in 1944, and by the spring of 1945 Japan's territorial control in the Pacific was collapsing as US and British Commonwealth forces advanced toward the home islands. Japanese leaders decided that the French colonial officials in Indochina were no longer useful and moved suddenly on 9 March to remove them. In an effort to gain cooperation from the Vietnamese, Tokyo recognized the heir of the Nguyen dynasty, Bao Dai, as emperor. Since neither the French nor Japanese had allowed the imperial court at Hue any real authority, this gesture had no political substance. When the Imperial Japanese Government announced its surrender to the Allies on 14 August, there was no effective government in place in Vietnam.

Although he had not anticipated the sudden Japanese capitulation, Ho immediately seized the moment. Signing his name one final time as Nguyen Ai Quoc, he issued a call to action: 'Dear fellow countrymen! The decisive hour has struck for the destiny of our people. ... Forward! Forward! Under the banner of the Viet Minh, let us valiantly march forward.'[14] In numerous towns and villages in Tonkin, Vietminh partisans easily claimed authority, and in Hanoi front forces under ICP leadership converged to take over government buildings from the Japanese. In Hue, Vietminh cadre entered the palace, and they demanded and received the abdication of Bao Dai. This August Revolution had been swift and bloodless.

On 2 September 1945, Ho Chi Minh stood on a platform in Hanoi's Ba Dinh Square before several thousand Vietnamese and some curious international observers, including members of the OSS. He undoubtedly got the attention of the Americans when he began his speech quoting the American Declaration of Independence: 'All men are created equal. They are endowed by their Creator with certain unalienable Rights; among these are Life, Liberty, and the pursuit of Happiness.' In this Vietnamese Declaration of Independence of a new Democratic Republic of Vietnam (DRV), Ho vowed 'to oppose the wicked schemes of the French imperialists' and he appealed to 'the victorious Allies to recognize our freedom and independence.'[15] Despite this bold rhetoric, the front that Ho led had only a few thousand members concentrated almost entirely in northern Vietnam. Among the 24 million Vietnamese there were other groups and potential leaders to challenge the ICP. By agreement among the Allies who fought Japan, British and Nationalist Chinese troops were poised to occupy Indochina and implement the

Japanese surrender. Most significantly, French forces were absent but were already en route back to reclaim their colony.

The Vietminh moved quickly to attempt to form a government. To appease traditionalists it gave an honorific but powerless office to Bao Dai. To hasten the departure of Chinese Nationalist troops from northern Vietnam, it promised some token representation in the DRV national assembly to remnants of the VNQDD and to the Dong Minh Hoi, two small factions that had received backing from the Guomindang. Once the Chinese were gone, it suppressed the small parties and conducted carefully staged elections in selected areas that gave the Vietminh almost unanimous control of the DRV assembly. In some cases, assassination took care of potentially troublesome rivals.

Vietminh followers in Saigon attempted an armed uprising to take control of the city as the front had done in Hanoi, but they lacked the numbers and discipline to be successful. As the semblance of a Vietnamese government appeared in the north, British forces occupied limited areas of Vietnam south of the sixteenth parallel. Acting largely on his own authority to curtail civilian casualties, British General Douglas Gracey supplemented his small command by arming French and even Japanese soldiers and suppressing the Vietminh in Saigon.

In October General Jacques Leclerc arrived in Saigon in command of the French Expeditionary Corps (FEC) to reclaim his country's colonial control. His limited forces grew gradually to about 50,000 men by the spring of 1946. He was able to occupy fairly quickly the principal population centers in southern Vietnam and Cambodia, to patrol some of the main communication routes, and, after six months, to place troops in Vientiane and Luang Prabang in Laos. Despite these seeming successes, Leclerc knew that there were large areas beyond French control, that the Vietminh was largely a nationalist movement, and that it would be difficult for France to prevail militarily. He privately urged Paris to try to reach a political settlement with the DRV.

A negotiated outcome appeared possible on 6 March. Jean Sainteny, serving in Hanoi as representative of France's High Commissioner for Indochina, Admiral Thierry d'Argenlieu, signed a preliminary convention with Ho Chi Minh. The document began: 'The French Government recognizes the Republic of Vietnam as a free state which has its government, its parliament, its army, and its finances, and is a part of the Indochinese Federation of the French Union.'[16] Both sides had made key concessions. The French offer of local autonomy within a federal system was a marked change from past practices. Ho had wanted recognition of an 'independent state' but settled for the ambiguous term 'free state.' Hopeful that he could secure more specific terms of agreement, Ho departed for France along with Pham Van Dong and others for continued talks.

On 30 May, d'Argenlieu dashed hopes of compromise when, on his own authority in Saigon, he recognized the Republic of Cochinchina, that is, the area of Saigon and the Mekong Delta, as a 'free state.' The admiral shared a belief common among many French officials, and contrary to that of Leclerc, that the Vietminh could not stand up to France's military power and hence that there was no reason to negotiate with the self-proclaimed DRV. At a formal conference at Fontainebleau in late summer, Pham Van Dong met a total rejection of any further concessions, and in the fall the Vietnamese delegation returned home empty handed. Inside Vietnam, the existence of rival Vietnamese states – the DRV in Tonkin and the French-backed creation in Cochinchina – inflamed emotions on both sides. Fear, mistrust, and occasional violence increased tensions. On 20 November, a clash between Vietminh troops and French naval patrol vessels in the port of Haiphong caused d'Argenlieu to order a punitive attack to send a message to the Vietnamese. French gunboats bombarded shore targets on 28 November 1945. Both sides magnified and distorted the initial clash and the effects of the Haiphong naval attack, and thereafter the Vietminh and French forces were in armed conflict. The Franco–Vietminh War had begun, and it would last eight years.

The French did not want a big war, and they never sent large numbers of troops to fight. The largest the FEC ever became was 192,000 in 1952, and the number of those troops who were European was less than 70,000. The remainder of the FEC was composed of French colonial soldiers from Africa or Indochina itself. French commanders expected their advantages over the Vietminh in weapons and technology would mean less need for ground forces. The FEC used the ports, roads, and railroads constructed during the colonial era as economic infrastructure to give it military access to the cities and towns, which it was able to occupy and control from Hanoi and Haiphong in the north to Danang and Saigon in the south. The French also used aerial warfare – high explosive bombs and incendiary bombs made of a jellied gasoline called napalm – to attempt to intimidate and crush the Vietminh fighters. In 1947 they launched some major offensives that created a lot of casualties, many of whom were civilians, but even that did not prompt concessions from the enemy. In fact, the destructiveness aided the Vietminh in convincing some Vietnamese of the necessity for fighting the FEC.[17]

The Vietminh strategy was to retreat away from the urban areas and to mount resistance from rural agricultural areas and the undeveloped mountains and marshes. The front created the People's Army of Vietnam (PAVN) headed by Vo Nguyen Giap. It organized a few conventional combat infantry divisions, but much of its military doctrine was based upon the concept of people's war developed by Mao Zedong and the Chinese Communist Party. The idea was to create remote base areas and to avoid fixed battles that allowed the enemy to use its technological and material advantages. Political cadres worked among the people to gain support, and military operations were primarily guerrilla harassment to drain enemy strength and undermine enemy morale. The theme for the fighters and the people was 'struggle' (*dau tranh*) or the notion that it would take time to develop a power equilibrium that would make possible a final and successful general offensive.[18]

By 1949 the war was becoming a stalemate, and the French realized they had to pay more attention to finding a Vietnamese political alternative to Ho Chi Minh and the Vietminh. France had control of urban areas, but it did not have the political will to commit resources to control the rural areas as well. For the French government, retaining Indochina was a matter of domestic and international pride and political credibility, but not of national survival. Moreover, any economic profit of the colony became null if colonial possession required a costly war and occupation. To save political face and keep some commercial access to the region, Paris tried what became known as the Bao Dai solution. On 8 March 1949 at Elysée, Bao Dai and the president of France signed agreements creating a single State of Vietnam with the former emperor as chief of state. The French agreed to dissolve the Republic of Cochinchina and to recognize the 'independence' of a single, undivided Vietnam with its capital in Saigon.[19]

Although bold in appearance, the Elysée agreements were a thinly veiled French political ploy. Although Bao Dai and other Vietnamese who distrusted and even feared the Vietminh entered into the plan earnestly and willingly, the agreements contained many pages of details that were far from a promise of independence. Also Bao Dai had no popular constituency with which to compete with Ho's patriotic front. When, on 1 July 1949, Bao Dai announced Ordinance Number One, the constitution of the State of Vietnam, there was no celebrating or even ceremony in Saigon as had occurred in Hanoi when Ho issued his declaration of independence. One thing was clear in 1949, however. Vietnam had in place two governments, each claiming to be the single government of the country. The DRV leadership was primarily from the

Indochina Communist Party and thus connected with other communist parties, and the State of Vietnam was led by Vietnamese who for reasons of tradition, ideology, or personal survival chose to identify with France and its international connections.

The United States and the Franco–Vietminh War

In 1950 the United States, which had emerged from the Second World War as the strongest nation in the world, economically and militarily, decided to involve itself in the Franco–Vietminh War. Before the Second World War, Washington treated Southeast Asia as a British and French sphere of interest, and any US strategic assessments of the value of the region were made in the context of the interests of America's European allies. Itself the product of a colonial war for independence, the United States had a historical tradition of opposition to colonialism that had been reaffirmed in President Woodrow Wilson's vision of the self-determination of nations. While critical of formal colonial annexation even as it governed the Philippines in the first part of the twentieth century, the United States as an industrial nation had pursued a practice, sometimes labeled informal empire, in which it worked to protect its own access to markets and raw materials in areas outside Europe and North America. In fact, the fracturing of British, French, and Dutch colonial systems in Southeast Asia during the Second World War and then the stopping of Japanese expansion seemed to serve US abstract criticism of colonialism and to open closed colonial areas to free trade. In some wartime discussions, President Franklin Roosevelt revealed his assumption that France was finished as an Asian power, and he spoke vaguely about some form of postwar trusteeship for Indochina. At the end of the war, the end of Western colonialism was a US policy objective, but political instability in Europe also meant that another key American objective was to maintain unity with its British and French allies. Roosevelt died in March 1945 leaving to his successor, Harry Truman, an ambiguous policy legacy in Indochina.[20]

Very quickly after the end of the world war, the defining US security interest became how to manage an increasingly hostile confrontation with the Soviet Union. This Cold War began in Europe as the Soviet government of Joseph Stalin sought to dictate the postwar political structure of Eastern Europe in order to protect the borders of the USSR and to gain control of the economic resources of the region. The United States had a different postwar vision of a politically and economically open Europe, and American leaders perceived Stalin's possessiveness as threatening and aggressive. Both sides defended their own positions in ideological terms, basically a conflict between capitalism and communism, that cast their differences in moral or theoretical absolutes that allowed little room for compromise and generalized their conflict to conditions throughout the world.

The Truman administration's strategy in the Cold War was containment, that is, the concept that any expansion of Soviet political or ideological influence anywhere was a threat to US security and must be opposed by comparable countermeasures. In the Truman Doctrine speech of March 1947, the president asked Congress to authorize US aid to Greece and Turkey to suppress communist insurrections. To convince his listeners, he pledged that the United States would aid any government threatened by 'totalitarianism,' the term he used to convey the communist threat.[21] The huge Marshall Plan of American economic assistance for Europe followed in June 1947, and the North Atlantic Treaty Organization (NATO) created in 1949 made US military forces integral to the military defense of Europe. The Truman administration had established a seemingly successful containment strategy in Europe that could be applied elsewhere. As the conflict in Indochina continued and appeared increasingly difficult for France to wage, its implications for the Cold War raised concern in Washington.

Although French colonialism held no attraction for US officials, France was an immensely important ally that was needed to maintain the solidarity of Western European defense against potential Soviet expansion. American leaders criticized the French for holding on to old imperial ambitions, but they would not risk an open break with Paris over the issue of Indochina. Moreover, US policy assumed that the communist ideology of the Soviet Union shared through a network of communist political organizations posed an inherent threat to US interests wherever it appeared. The Vietminh was led by an Asian communist known to have worked for many years with the Comintern as a party organizer. When Paris turned to the Bao Dai solution, it was not only trying to appeal to traditional Vietnamese people, it was also seeking to gain US assistance in a joint effort to provide a noncommunist alternative in Vietnam to the communist Ho Chi Minh.

In October 1949 with the establishment of the People's Republic of China, the Chinese Communist Party proclaimed victory after years of struggle with the Nationalist Party. The appearance of a major communist-led state bordering on Vietnam brought the logic of the containment strategy to Asia. In geopolitical terms, the possible spread of ideologically connected communist political systems from China into Southeast Asia seemed to parallel the perceived danger of possible Soviet expansionism from Eastern to Western Europe. Thus Vietnam began to assume importance as a strategic location for the containment of communism. The creation of the State of Vietnam allowed French officials to declare that their country was fighting a war for containment, not for colonization. This assertion of a need to counter the creation of a communist bloc in Asia appeared to be validated in January 1950 when the new government in Beijing extended diplomatic recognition to the Democratic Republic of Vietnam. Despite the history of Chinese–Vietnamese antagonism, Ho and the ICP decided to accept military and economic aid from the PRC as a means of achieving their immediate objective of defeating the French.

In addition to seeing a strategic value in helping France in Vietnam in terms of preserving good relations within the European alliance and checking the spread of Chinese Communist influence in Asia, the United States also had economic reasons to aid France. Mainland Southeast Asia was not a significant market or source of raw materials for the United States, but it was important in those respects to America's allies Britain and France. Southeast Asia was also a natural economic partner for an industrialized Japan, which had tried unsuccessfully to control access to the region by force during the Pacific war. With China a communist state, foreign policy analysts in the United States began to plan for the economic development of a pacified Japan as a strategic and economic benefit. For France, Britain, and Japan to be political allies and trading partners of the United States, preserving French interests in Indochina became part of America's global security planning.

Based upon these calculations of US interest, Washington recognized the State of Vietnam on 7 February 1950. In May the Truman administration offered $10 million in support of the French military effort and created a US Military Assistance Advisory Group (MAAG) in Saigon. At the time these steps seemed small and gave no indication that they were the beginning of what would be 25 years of direct American military and diplomatic engagement in Indochina. They were undertaken, however, as part of a response to what appeared to be a mounting global crisis. In late 1949 the Soviet Union successfully tested an atomic bomb, and soon afterward much publicized espionage cases, such as the trials of Julius and Ethel Rosenberg and of Alger Hiss, further heightened American concerns about Soviet aggression. In February 1950 Senator Joseph McCarthy began making disturbing, although unsubstantiated, allegations of extensive communist infiltration of the US State

Department. Deliberations within the National Security Council produced a top-secret report, NSC-68, in April 1950 that established a policy of preparing the United States for the armed containment of communism throughout the world. When North Korean forces crossed the thirty-eighth parallel into South Korea in June 1950 leading to the Korean War, the logic and prudence of US military assistance to the Republic of Korea and the State of Vietnam seemed confirmed.[22]

Despite the connections that US officials made between the hostilities in Asia and a worldwide communist danger, they sought to keep the American military role in Asia limited. The principal battleground of the Cold War was Europe, and the Truman administration did not want to commit the full strength of American resources to conflicts outside of Europe. Especially after the PRC entered the Korean War in late 1950, Washington's determination to avoid a wider war in Asia increased. American strategists were unwilling to recognize the communist-led Vietminh as the champions of the historic Vietnamese quest for national unity and independence, but they urged the French to give Bao Dai's government greater freedom in order to strengthen it politically and make it less dependent on external support. Although Paris welcomed US assistance, it spurned US advice.

In 1950–52, the FEC fought major battles with the Vietminh and suffered heavy losses. Washington continued to conclude that it had no choice but to stick with the French and their Bao Dai solution, and thus American aid increased in order to sustain the French effort. The Truman administration was trying to convince Paris to support American defense plans for Western Europe, including possible rearmament of West Germany (a thought abhorrent to many in France), and continued aid to the war in Indochina became in effect hostage to that effort. Also, as the war dragged on in a bloody stalemate, it was becoming increasingly controversial within France. Washington did not want Paris to abandon its war against the Vietminh and present a situation in which the United States might have to attempt military containment alone in Vietnam while the war in Korea continued and defense of Europe remained paramount. Consequently, by 1953 the level of US aid had risen to the point that it was more than one-third of the French war costs.[23]

When the Truman presidency ended in 1953, the Vietnam War was not an American war. For the Vietminh it was a war for liberation from French colonial claims. For France it was a war to regain prestige and imperial power after the humiliation of the German occupation during the Second World War. For the United States a Vietminh victory would provide an unacceptable strategic gain for America's adversaries in the Cold War. From the American perspective, the continuation of French colonialism was also undesired, and the colonial nature of the war restrained US involvement. A communist success in Vietnam could not be tolerated, however, because it would threaten the security of US inter- ests in Europe and Asia. The Truman administration was aiding France but was not fighting the Vietminh directly. US policy decisions had defined Indochina as strategically important, but those decisions had not yet committed the United States to the Vietnam War.

2
Commitments: Dwight D. Eisenhower, John F. Kennedy, and Ngo Dinh Diem

Over the decade from 1953 to 1963, US policy toward Vietnam moved from a measured containment approach to an avowed commitment to the survival of the Republic of Vietnam in the south as a global strategic imperative. The colonial origins of the French war, doubts about Paris's ability to prevail, and the historically marginal nature of US interests in Southeast Asia initially restrained the American involvement. The Truman administration wanted no American war in Vietnam, but was willing to aid France in Indochina for reasons of keeping good relations with a NATO ally and because of regional security concerns in Asia. In January 1953 Dwight D. Eisenhower became president, and US policy continued to concentrate on aid to France's war effort. After little more than a year, however, Paris decided to end its almost eight-year quest to subdue the Vietminh by force. Unwilling to concede the region to communist-led political regimes, Washington chose to seek a strategic outpost in South Vietnam and provided US aid directly to Vietnamese opponents of the Democratic Republic of Vietnam (DRV). The Eisenhower administration identified Ngo Dinh Diem as the best available leader of this effort. By 1961 when John F. Kennedy entered the White House, Diem's American-backed government in Saigon remained extremely insecure. The new administration increased the US commitment to its ally. The level of US economic and military aid and the number of American military personnel grew significantly. At the time Kennedy and Diem fell victim to assassination in November 1963, the United States remained firmly committed to preventing unification of Vietnam under the DRV.

The end of the Franco–Vietminh War

In February 1953, Eisenhower addressed Congress for the first time as president. He chose to characterize the French war against the Vietminh as holding 'the line of freedom' against 'Communist aggression throughout the world.'[1] General Eisenhower had served under Truman as commander of all NATO forces and shared the official estimates in Washington that the areas of freedom in the world were under assault from a 'Communist-regimented unity.'[2] Throughout his eight years in the White House he did not waver in his view that there was a global struggle between freedom and tyranny and that the conflict in Southeast Asia was central to that fight. In January 1961, as he prepared for the transition in power to president-elect John Kennedy, he issued a final statement, a farewell address, in which he warned that the United States and its allies would continue to face 'a hostile ideology – global in scope, atheistic in character, ruthless in purpose, and insidious in method.'[3]

The general who had led the allied forces in the liberation of Nazi-occupied Europe during the Second World War would accept no compromise with world communism, but as the Republican candidate for president he also made a commitment to American voters that he would reduce government costs, including expenditures for national defense. In contrast to the previous administration that greatly increased military spending, Eisenhower's advisers developed a New Look strategy whose premise was to find the most economical ways to protect American security. One was to get 'more bang for the buck' by threatening use of nuclear force to deter aggression. In addition to this doctrine of 'massive retaliation,' the New Look also included expanding the number of regional military alliances and making greater use of covert operations.[4] In Indochina, the New Look approach meant, at least initially, that the United States would continue to work in partnership with France to prevent a Vietminh victory that would mean a success for international communism.

Eisenhower and his aides were as opposed as had been previous American administrations to the French objective to restore colonial rule to Indochina, but the containment strategy still required the United States to hold ranks with its NATO ally. Eisenhower's secretary of state, John Foster Dulles, explained privately to the Senate Foreign Relations Committee that the current division within the world left no alternative but to accept continued French influence in Indochina in order to prevent Soviet and Chinese gains in Southeast Asia.[5] Dulles was also trying to convince French leaders to accept a plan known as the European Defense Community (EDC), which would strengthen NATO's position by rearming West Germany. Such a move was politically very sensitive in France, and American aid in Indochina was viewed as part of the inducement to gain Paris's acceptance of the EDC. In addition, France appointed a new commander of the French Expeditionary Corps (FEC) in 1953, General Henri Navarre, who presented a plan to the Americans to increase the size of the Vietnamese National Army of the State of Vietnam, to give more independence to states of the French Union, and to be more aggressive in combating the Vietminh. To support the Navarre Plan and to buttress the EDC talks, the Eisenhower administration increased US military assistance to a level that provided almost 80 percent of France's military expenditures in Indochina by January 1954.[6]

Despite Navarre's élan and the show of US support, French public and official opinion was turning against what many in France called 'the dirty war.' France had endured more than seven years of death and expense, and the will of the Vietminh to continue to die and struggle was undiminished. Consequently and against the desires of Washington, French premier Joseph Laniel accepted a Soviet proposal for an international conference in Geneva, Switzerland, to seek possible diplomatic settlements in Korea and Indochina. Scheduled to begin in April 1954, the Geneva Conference would include representatives not only of France and the DRV but also the United States, United Kingdom, Soviet Union (USSR), and the People's Republic of China (PRC). Dulles opposed the idea of compromise with communists, but believed that to oppose the meeting could prompt a unilateral French withdrawal from the war. He was also still seeking French approval of the EDC and did not wish to alienate Paris for the sake of that initiative.

With the prospects looming of a possible settlement or cease-fire, attention turned to a remote village in northwestern Vietnam, Dienbienphu, the site of what became the decisive military engagement of the Franco–Vietminh War. In late 1953 Navarre began construction of a fortified base at Dienbienphu on the floor of a mountain valley. Although he thought this camp would strengthen the FEC in the area, Navarre seriously underestimated the ability of the usually elusive Vietminh to challenge such a fixed position. Aware that a dramatic military success would greatly enhance their negotiating position at Geneva, the Vietminh began preparing for a conventional attack. On 13 March, the People's Army of Vietnam led by Vo Nguyen Giap assaulted the entrenched French garrison with artillery and infantry and cut it off from resupply and reenforcement. A French military disaster appeared likely, and the ultimate result could be a complete French diplomatic capitulation at Geneva.

A French defeat at the hands of the Vietminh had serious negative implications for US containment objectives. It would mean territorial and political gains for an ally of the Soviet Union and the PRC. Moreover the United States had openly supported France and the Bao Dai solution, and French failure could cause US allies and adversaries in Asia and Europe to question American effectiveness in international affairs. American leaders began to consider use of the New Look's principal deterrent – massive retaliation. Although some contingency plans for use of nuclear weapons in Indochina existed, American strategists did not think atomic bombs were needed to break the Vietminh encirclement of Dienbienphu. The proposed form of US intervention, eventually code named Operation Vulture, was a massive bombing of Vietminh positions with conventional high explosives dropped from as many as 350 planes flying from US aircraft carriers in the Gulf of Tonkin and from airbases in Okinawa and the Philippines.[7]

On 20 March, General Paul Ely, chairman of the French Chiefs of Staff, came to Washington with a carefully worded request for an air strike and implied that without such help France would likely have to withdraw its forces from Vietnam. For several weeks Eisenhower and his chief aides weighed the idea of bombing but never approved it. On 7 May, the French garrison surrendered after sustaining heavy losses, and this outcome set the stage for the signing of a cease-fire agreement between France and the Vietminh at Geneva in July. The US decision not to intervene militarily at the decisive stage of the war has attracted considerable attention from historians.

In late March and April as the administration decided on its course of action, Eisenhower and Dulles publicly affirmed the importance the United States placed on the outcome in Indochina. On 29 March Dulles delivered a carefully drafted speech asserting that Indochina was of 'great strategic value,' and he called on other nations for 'united action' against the Vietminh.[8] In response to a reporter's question on 7 April, Eisenhower cited the 'falling domino' principle that a Vietminh victory could set off a sequence of events threatening all of Southeast Asia and even Japan, Taiwan, the Philippines, Australia, and New Zealand. 'The possible consequences of the loss are just incalculable to the free world,' he concluded.[9]

Behind the scenes, the president and secretary of state worked to arrange a political and diplomatic foundation for intervention. Dulles met privately with congressional leaders, who preferred multilateral action. Eisenhower wrote directly to British prime minister Winston Churchill seeking joint action, but the elder statesman and his aides chose to await developments at Geneva. In subsequent public statements, the White House conveyed the image that its hands were tied by congressional and allied reluctance to attempt a risky rescue of France's failed adventure. This image making proved to be good domestic politics because it protected Eisenhower later from personal attacks that he had 'lost Vietnam' – avoiding the kind of criticism that Truman had endured for the 'loss of China' when the Chinese Communist Party triumphed there in 1949.

Some scholars have pointed to America's Dienbienphu decisions as evidence of Eisenhower's effective leadership. Indochina presented a military-diplomatic problem to which the president could with confidence apply his personal experience. In their public statements, key officials such as Dulles and Vice-President Richard M. Nixon raised the possibility of using the US military in Vietnam, but the president made the decision to keep American ground and air forces out of combat. He told his aides: 'It would be a great mistake for the United States to enter the fray in partnership only with France. ... United action by the free world was necessary, and in such action the U.S. role would not require use of its ground troops.'[10] This prudent assessment stands in apparent contrast to the actions of later presidents who led US forces into hostile action in Southeast Asia.[11] Eisenhower's caution, however, arose from the immediate weakness of the French position and a judgment that Paris had lost the will to fight. His administration had not changed US purposes in Vietnam. Dienbienphu was a momentary setback in the Cold War in Asia, but Eisenhower continued to believe that Indochina was an important location in the global balance of power.[12]

Following the Vietminh success at Dienbienphu, it became likely that France would accept a compromise settlement at Geneva. Not wanting to be party to any agreement recognizing the legitimacy of the DRV, the Eisenhower administration elected to observe the Geneva proceedings and not actively engage in arranging terms. The United States maintained a presence there, however, because its leaders were not eager to take a unilateral course in the region. With Britain, the USSR, and the PRC urging both sides to make accommodations, the French and Vietminh agreed to a cease-fire with the DRV controlling the area north of the seventeenth parallel and France regrouping the FEC south of that line. This military disengagement plan created a temporary partition between North Vietnam and South Vietnam. A separate, unsigned declaration issued at the end of the conference on 21 July 1954 emphasized that the military demarcation line was not a political or territorial boundary. In other words, the Geneva Agreements did not resolve the issue of governing authority within Vietnam and called for 'free general elections' throughout Vietnam in July 1956 to determine the future political structure of the nation. The US representatives issued a statement acknowledging, but not endorsing these terms.[13]

The US decision to support South Vietnam

The day after the Geneva Conference adjourned, the National Security Council met in Washington to survey the damage. Dulles set out the next step for US policy: 'The remaining free areas of Indochina must be built up if the dike against Communism is to be held.'[14] One of the first US actions was to put into effect the 'united action' formula for which the secretary of state had appealed in March during the siege of Dienbienphu. Washington began diplomatic exchanges that led to the creation of the Southeast Asia Treaty Organization (SEATO) in September 1954. Also known as the Manila Pact for the city where it was signed, it was a regional defense alliance of the United States, France, Britain, Australia, New Zealand, the Philippines, Thailand, and Pakistan. Although the name purposely invited parallels with NATO, this treaty did not commit its members to specific responses as was the case with NATO, but it did provide for consultation to arrange joint action in a crisis like Dienbienphu and especially in case of overt aggression by the PRC or North Vietnam directed at a Southeast Asian state. Although the Geneva cease-fire terms prohibited Vietnam, Laos, and Cambodia from joining military alliances, the SEATO pact included a protocol defining these countries as part of the 'treaty area.' Satisfied with the treaty, Dulles described it as a 'no trespassing' sign to deter communist aggressors, and Eisenhower and the presidents who followed him invoked SEATO as their authority for American intervention in Southeast Asian affairs.[15]

The care that Eisenhower took to keep the United States apart from the substantive negotiations and final agreements at Geneva helped him escape political criticism that he had compromised with communists – an allegation that some Republicans had made against Franklin Roosevelt after the Yalta Conference of 1945. American public opinion favored toughness in US policies toward communist regimes, but not at the risk of war. The administration's aloofness at Geneva and its leadership in the creation of SEATO fit the public mood. By itself, however, toughness was not a sufficient policy. The White House had decided not to resort to military force in Indochina but was also unwilling to recognize the *de facto* reality of DRV military and political success. The French war suggested two options: either apply more force against the Vietminh or seek a basis on which to negotiate with it. In the wake of France's decision to quit the war, Washington was contemplating deepening the US commitment to prevent further DRV success, but was not inclined to examine the lessons of the French experience.[16]

France had joined SEATO because the region remained important to the Europeans, but the Eisenhower administration had largely dismissed the French as a factor in the future of Vietnam. Eisenhower and other senior US officials thought that Paris had suffered a failure of political will against the Vietminh. They viewed the French defeat as a measure of French weakness rather than DRV strength. The president confided to a close friend that he was tired of the French and their 'seemingly hysterical desire to be thought such a "great power."'[17] The French presence remained strong in Vietnam, however, and Paris was not ready to relinquish the economic and personal connections that it still had.

To jump start the American plan to sustain the State of Vietnam in the French regroupment zone south of the demarcation line, Eisenhower sent General J. Lawton Collins to Saigon in November 1954. 'Lightning Joe' Collins had served as one of Eisenhower's principal field commanders in the Second World War, spoke French, and was personally acquainted with General Ely, who had been appointed French high commissioner in Indochina. Designated as the president's personal representative, Collins had instructions to formulate 'a crash program' to maintain a government in Saigon and to 'establish security in Free Vietnam.' The president expected French officials in Saigon to cooperate, but, if not, he was ready 'to lay down the law to the French.' 'It is true that we have to cajole the French with regard to the European area,' he told the National Security Council, 'but we certainly didn't have to in Indochina.'[18]

The principal challenge facing Collins, as it had French officials in Vietnam, was to identify and sustain a Vietnamese leader who could compete with Ho Chi Minh and around whom a regime friendly to Western interests could be built. In June 1954 while the Geneva Conference was underway, Bao Dai had appointed Ngo Dinh Diem prime minister of the State of Vietnam. Although the FEC was the controlling authority south of the seventeenth parallel, it was the government that Diem headed that would have to face the DRV in the 1956 election stipulated by the final declaration at Geneva. The Vietminh had enormous political appeal after the heroic victory at Dienbienphu and the diplomatic recognition that the DRV received at Geneva. Many Vietnamese knew the Vietminh's reputation for ruthlessness, however, and hoped for a different nationalist leader. The new Diem administration was unproven in its ability, and Bao Dai had the image of being a French puppet. American officials were still trying to decide what they thought of Diem, but they believed that his only chance to succeed would be if the French gave him an independence of action that Paris had in the past denied to Bao Dai's cabinets.

French officials in Paris and Saigon did not like Diem and let the Americans know it. As a young man, Diem had resigned in 1933 from a position at the court in Hue when he realized that the colonial rulers were not going to allow the similarly youthful emperor Bao Dai any meaningful authority. For similar reasons he declined to accept a cabinet position from Bao Dai in 1949. Among Vietnamese he had a reputation for independence, honesty, and courageous criticism of French rule. The Vietminh viewed Diem and the closely knit Ngo family as potential rivals. Reportedly, the Vietminh assassinated the oldest Ngo brother, Ngo Dinh Khoi, soon after the September 1945 revolution and later threatened Diem with assassination.

Diem was both anticommunist and anticolonialist, qualities that clearly coincided with US policies in Indochina. Unfortunately for American strategists, however, he lacked the charisma and political skills usually associated with political leadership. He projected a mandarin's reserve toward the common people, and he had no personal political following. He could count on the support of his politically savvy brothers, but their clannishness made people wary. The Ngos were Roman Catholics, which provided some affinity with their coreligionists but which also set them apart from the majority of Vietnamese who were at least nominally Buddhist. Diem was personally quite devout and at various times had considered becoming a priest.

Bao Dai disliked and distrusted Diem, and his decision to appoint Diem prime minister in June 1954 was surprising. Partly to avoid Vietminh assassins, Diem had resided for a time in the United States in the early 1950s, and he had met some prominent Americans, including Senator Mike Mansfield and Francis Cardinal Spellman, the archbishop of New York. It is possible that some hidden maneuvering by Americans, possibly through the Central Intelligence Agency (CIA), may have led Bao Dai to select Diem, but there is no clear-cut historical evidence that this was the case. It is more likely that Bao Dai on his own turned to Diem as a means of trying to win US backing for the State of Vietnam as the French were at Geneva negotiating a possible exit from Indochina.[19]

Collins arrived in Saigon in November with specific instructions from Eisenhower to make a judgment of Diem's ability to provide the alternative regime Washington desired to contest the communist-led DRV. Weeks earlier, CIA director Allan Dulles, the secretary of state's brother, had already sent to South Vietnam his own representative to work with Diem – Colonel Edward G. Lansdale, an air force officer who had secretly aided Philippine president Ramon Magsaysay in politically outmaneuvering communist insurgents. Lansdale befriended Diem and provided him political advice. Although Lansdale maintained that what Diem needed was unqualified US backing and not American criticism, Collins reported after being in Vietnam for five months that Diem was incapable of providing the strong leadership that South Vietnam needed. In the general's opinion, the regime in Saigon was a 'practically one-man government' that had to be substantially broadened to include other patriotic Vietnamese who opposed the communists. Having visited Vietnam and gained a favorable impression of Diem and having received Lansdale's reports affirming Diem's potential, Secretary of State Dulles was unprepared for Collins's negative assessment.[20]

In April 1955 Collins returned from Saigon for face-to-face meetings with Dulles and State Department officials to decide the US position toward Diem. The general stood firm on his recommendation. From these meetings came a formal decision for 'some change in political arrangements in Viet-Nam' away from US support of Diem and to coop-eration with alternative South Vietnamese leaders.[21] Before the policy could be implemented, however, fighting erupted in Saigon on 28 April that prompted Washington to delay acting. Armed units organized by various religious sects in the South and by gangsters who controlled the vice trade in Saigon battled elements of the Vietnamese National Army. As Collins hurried back to Saigon, the troops supporting Diem quelled this so-called sect uprising. Although firm evidence is illusive, Lansdale may have been a central figure in both the timing of the start of the fight-ing and in arranging the critical military defense of the prime minister. Dulles's Asian advisers argued that the crisis atmosphere and Diem's ability, at least for the moment, to survive made the time inopportune for applying pressure for internal political changes. They convinced the secretary of state to reverse the decision reached when Collins was in Washington and to make wholehearted support of Diem the basis of US policy. It cannot be known if a shift to some other South Vietnamese leader in 1955 would have changed the ultimate course of the Vietnam War, but from that point until 1963 the success of US objectives in Vietnam depended on the ability of Diem to create an effective government.[22]

The Eisenhower administration's decision to continue to work with Diem as the best hope for sustaining a regime in South Vietnam separate from the DRV placed further strain on US–French cooperation in the region. French officials knew that Diem was not amenable to their influence, and they persisted in portraying him as unfit to lead in an effort to undermine the American view that he deserved a chance to form a government. In early May 1955, Dulles held several meetings in Paris with French premier Edgar Faure. They could not reach agreement, but finally Faure acquiesced to Dulles's insistence on Diem.[23] The French government reached the point where it no longer wished to contest the Eisenhower administration over the direction of Western policy in Vietnam. Over the next few months, it withdrew the FEC from the country and left the building of a nation in South Vietnam to the Americans.

Nation building in South Vietnam

Washington had taken a major step toward deeper involvement in the internal affairs of Southeast Asia, but the process toward what eventually became an American war was not yet inevitable. With SEATO, the possibility existed of collective international action to sustain South Vietnam, but France's decision to withdraw the FEC meant that external assistance to Saigon now would be largely a unilateral American program. The big question was whether Diem could be effective even with US help. The Eisenhower administration had set for itself a challenge to build a viable Vietnamese nation in the south.

Nation building faced major obstacles. As head of the State of Vietnam, Bao Dai provided little legitimacy. Although he was the heir of the Nguyen Dynasty, the monarchy had been moribund for decades, and Bao Dai himself lived a self-indulgent life on the French Riviera. The Vietnamese National Army consisted of about 150,000 soldiers led by officers whom the French military had never given combat leadership or any type of command experience. Similarly, Vietnamese civilians who had worked in the colonial bureaucracy were accustomed to taking orders and were not experienced in running agencies or planning programs. South Vietnam had basically no industrial capacity. Although rice and rubber were agricultural products with significant revenue potential, years of absentee landlordism, plantation farming, high taxes, and other colonial practices left a population of poor, debt-ridden farmers with no consumer-spending capacity and with no affinity for the Saigon government tainted by its past connections with the French.[24]

Given enough time, the Diem government could seek to correct its weak leadership structure and lack of a popular political base, but the Geneva Accords had set July 1956 as a date for elections that would pit this struggling regime against the disciplined DRV leadership and its claim to be national liberators. A genuinely free election would doubtlessly have resulted in a victory for Ho Chi Minh as president of a unified Vietnam, and hence neither Saigon nor Washington wanted it to occur. Vietnam had never in its history had a free national election, however, and the diplomats at Geneva had not proposed a specific voting process or even ballot for 1956. There was no possibility that the two Vietnamese sides would cooperate on fashioning an election, and none of the major Geneva participants – Britain, France, the Soviet Union, and China – pressed for a vote.[25]

When no election planning had begun by the summer of 1955, a national vote was essentially a dead letter, but Diem's leadership remained extremely tenuous. His constitutional authority as prime minister came from Bao Dai, whose own position was understood throughout Vietnam to have been created by France. US officials worried that, as long as the State of Vietnam remained burdened with this image as a puppet regime, it would not be able to compete politically with the nationalist appeal of the DRV.[26] As he had done when he managed to suppress the sect uprising in the spring, Diem surprised Washington in October 1955 by suddenly announcing and easily winning a referendum that deposed Bao Dai and made Diem president of a newly created Republic of Vietnam (RVN). In the balloting, Diem received 98 percent of the votes. The outcome was not evidence of an outpouring of popular support but rather of the ability of the Ngo family, especially Diem's younger brothers Ngo Dinh Nhu and Ngo Dinh Can, to manipulate ballots. Although Lansdale had warned the Ngos not to be overzealous in ensuring the victory, Diem and his American supporters now cited the election as a basis for the regime's authority.[27]

The lopsided election was only one indicator, however, of an emerging family dictatorship in South Vietnam. Diem's brothers Nhu and Can led a secret political organization, the Can Lao, that used a combination of threats and bribes to build support for Diem within the military and bureaucracy. In another rigged election in March 1956, the RVN chose a constituent assembly to draft a constitution with extensive executive powers. In October the president issued an ordinance replacing elected village councils with village chiefs selected by the central government. Individuals considered to be disloyal to the regime were arrested as Vietminh 'suspects' and sent to 'reeducation camps.' Secretary Dulles and some other American leaders rationalized this behavior as consistent with traditional Asian concepts of centralized authority and as necessary steps to give the RVN the security to develop more orderly procedures. Collins had warned that Diem and his family worked primarily to protect themselves and not to build a politically integrated regime. Washington chose, however, to assure Diem of wholehearted support and continued providing material aid to the RVN without due regard for its undemocratic and repressive actions.[28]

The United States provided almost a quarter of a billion dollars per year to South Vietnam during the second half of the 1950s. This sum was enormous for that time. A small portion of this aid went into economic development ideas that did little to address systemic changes. In rural areas some rent controls and land transfer plans were announced, but most were not implemented. In urban areas, an import-subsidy program made some consumer goods, such as electrical appliances, more available, creating a false impression of economic improvement without strengthening the economic infrastructure.[29] Eighty percent of US aid, however, went directly to the South Vietnamese armed forces because the Eisenhower administration considered military security to be the most urgent need of the Saigon government. Eisenhower did not deploy US combat troops to Vietnam, and the number of uniformed American advisors in the RVN was never more than 900 before 1961. On the other hand, US funds paid for 85 percent of the cost of maintaining the 150,000 soldiers of the Army of the Republic of Vietnam (ARVN).[30]

South Vietnam had a repressive government that was highly dependent on US aid, but in May 1957 the Eisenhower administration staged a major public relations event to portray Diem and the RVN as a great success. During a state visit to Washington, Diem attended elegant dinners, met privately with Eisenhower and Dulles in the White House, and addressed a joint session of Congress. This ceremonial treatment was intended to strengthen Diem's image as a leader. It was one of several such state visits hosted by Eisenhower for Asian and African leaders as part of a wider effort to improve US relations with the so-called Third World.[31] Publicly Eisenhower and other official spokesmen hailed Diem as a 'tough miracle man' and the 'savior' of South Vietnam.[32] They characterized his regime as an important partner with the United States in the fight against global communism. Privately the official talks were cordial but more cautious. Eisenhower refused Diem's request for a higher level of aid on the grounds that American commitments worldwide prevented greater assistance. Eisenhower reassured Diem that the United States continued to define South Vietnam as strategically important, and he renewed the pledge of wholehearted support of Diem that Dulles had made in 1955.[33]

As the administration formulated a US commitment to the survival of a separate, noncommunist regime in Vietnam, Congress and the public accepted this policy as part of containment. During the Dienbienphu deliberations, congressional leaders such as Senator Lyndon B. Johnson of Texas had cautioned against unilateral intervention, but did not question the strategic value of Vietnam. The US commitment to Diem also received nonpartisan political support from a group of prominent citizens called the American Friends of Vietnam. It included a number of members of Congress, among them Senator John F. Kennedy of Massachusetts, who in a speech to the organization described South Vietnam as the 'finger in the dike' that was holding back 'the red tide of Communism' in Southeast Asia.[34] Despite this rhetorical importance given Vietnam, however, the president and Congress were determined to limit the US commitment to a level that was economically manageable. The nuclear arms race with the Soviet Union escalated with the Soviet launch of the Sputnik space satellite in 1957, big-power tension continued over flash points such as Berlin and Korea, and a political revolution appeared on America's doorstep in Cuba. These challenges meant that Washington had to measure out its national security resources carefully.

During Eisenhower's second term beginning in 1957 US foreign aid budgets shrank, but in South Vietnam America's Diem experiment faced growing difficulty. Saigon's steps to suppress opposition were leading to mounting incidents of terrorism and antigovernment violence in retaliation. Although Hanoi wanted the RVN to fail and remained determined to unite Vietnam under DRV rule, Communist Party leaders in the north initially ordered their cadre in the south to avoid force and employ propaganda and political recruiting to organize resistance to Diem's rule. Hanoi's strategists did not want an armed conflict that might risk a US military retaliation on North Vietnam while the regime there was still consolidating its control. Southern resistance fighters were feeling the sting of harsh punishments, including executions, however, and would not remain passive. Without orders they resorted to assassination, arson, and harassing attacks on ARVN units.[35]

In trying to respond to these pressures, US and RVN officials sharply disagreed over how to use the American aid. Serving essentially as his brother's chief of staff, Ngo Dinh Nhu insisted that available funds go almost entirely to military assistance to expand and better arm the ARVN. The US ambassador in Saigon, Elbridge Durbrow, countered that US aid should address the heart of the problem of building popular support for the regime by fostering economic improvements and political reform. Durbrow even suggested to Washington that the threat of withholding military supplies be used to pressure the Ngos into implementation of land reform, press freedom, and other measures that could reduce public discontent.[36]

Despite the logic of Durbrow's recommendation, his get-tough approach to the Ngos ran counter to the concept of wholehearted support of Saigon and met strong resistance from some officials. Assigned to the Pentagon in Washington with the rank of brigadier general, Lansdale complained that Durbrow's attitude toward Diem was 'insulting, misinformed, and unfriendly.'[37] The commander of the US Military Assistance Advisory Group in Vietnam, Lieutenant General Samuel T. Williams, expressed disbelief that the ambassador would dare to deny essential military supplies to the RVN when it was facing armed and brutal opponents. In his view these enemies had to be destroyed before economic and political reform would be possible. Williams and Lansdale maintained that Diem needed reassurance not criticism, but Durbrow and others in the State Department contended that Diem was not beyond reproach. Recalling Diem's somewhat surprising political survival in 1955 with timely US assistance, Durbrow informed Washington that the United States faced a 'more complicated situation in the case of the GVN [Government of Vietnam] and that we have left the "Lansdale days" behind.'[38] The emotions of the ambassador and the generals evident in this debate demonstrated the importance that they all assigned to US interests in Vietnam. No one recommended reconsideration of the American commitment to South Vietnam. In the end the administration did not threaten Diem and continued to provide primarily military aid at the existing level.

While the Americans weighed their course, decisions were being reached in Hanoi. In January 1959 the Central Committee of the Vietnam Workers Party (the name adopted by the Vietnamese division of the Indochina Communist Party in 1951) passed a resolution accepting 'protracted armed struggle' to 'overthrow the US–Diem regime.'[39] In May the DRV formed a secret organization to begin building a system of trails – eventually known as the Ho Chi Minh Trail – to transport troops, weapons, and supplies from the north through Laos into the

Central Highlands of South Vietnam. The pace of the insurgency in the south quickened. On 20 December 1960 at a hidden location in Tay Ninh province northwest of Saigon, party organizers created a new patriotic front strikingly similar to the old Vietminh organization. Welcoming all Vietnamese who opposed imperialism and feudalism, the National Liberation Front (NLF) of South Vietnam was composed largely of southern insurgents working in cooperation with the DRV. Thus the threat that the RVN faced from the NLF was neither civil war nor external aggression alone; it was both.

In January 1961, only a few days after the secret founding of the NLF and a few days before Eisenhower would relinquish his office to president-elect John Kennedy, Lansdale delivered a warning in Washington based upon personal observations he made in Vietnam in December. He reported that the RVN was in 'critical condition' and that the Vietnamese communists (whom Diem and his officers called 'Vietcong') 'have started to steal the country and expect to be done in 1961.'[40] In a national security briefing for his successor, Eisenhower called direct attention to the containment of communism in Southeast Asia, although he focused his remarks on civil war in Laos in which the United States and the Soviet Union were supplying competing sides. In Eisenhower's opinion, the SEATO Treaty required the United States to act to defend the region.

After an initial period of joint action with France and shaping a collective defense mechanism with SEATO, the Eisenhower administration after the spring of 1955 had established a unilateral and increasingly firm commitment to building an independent nation in South Vietnam around Ngo Dinh Diem. If the southern regime proved able to survive only with US help, it could become in effect a neocolonial American dependent, which would leave the DRV able to claim the role of champion of national independence. Although some American officials raised this concern, the policy of wholehearted support for Diem continued and had become firmly entrenched in US containment strategy by the end of Eisenhower's presidency.

After the Franco–Vietminh War ended with the Geneva cease-fire agreements, the issue in Vietnam through the rest of the decade was not military strategy but internal political and economic development. During Diem's state visit to the United States in 1957, Eisenhower had joined with Dulles and others in praise of Diem's achievements, but beneath the miracle facade there were serious problems. The RVN government had a very narrow political base, its military structure was weak, South Vietnam's economy was undeveloped, and armed insurgency was growing. Eisenhower left Kennedy a policy of unequivocal support of Diem that had kept the domino from falling, but had not produced a self-sufficient nation in the south. Even worse from the US perspective was that the threat posed by the NLF presented the possible collapse of America's eight-year effort if the level and substance of American assistance remained the same.

John F. Kennedy and counterinsurgency warfare

When John F. Kennedy became president of the United States on 20 January 1961, the policy of building a South Vietnamese nation to contain the spread of communism in Southeast Asia was failing. Neither Truman's containment policy nor Eisenhower's nurturing of Diem had given sufficient weight to Vietnamese nationalism. Washington's global calculations of American, Soviet, and Chinese power did not adequately account for domestic realities in Vietnam. Diem was an antiforeign nationalist who hated the French, resented his dependence on the Americans, and took great pride in the tradition of Vietnamese resistance to Chinese domination. He frequently lectured visiting Americans for hours about the history of his country. His antiforeignism did not translate into political popularity, however, because his arrogant manner, clannishness, and Catholicism weakened his ability to compete with the charismatic Ho Chi Minh and the disciplined cadres of the NLF and DRV.

Kennedy entered the White House convinced of the importance of the so-called 'Third World' in the Cold War conflict. As a Democratic candidate for president, he had criticized the Republican Eisenhower administration for lack of vigor in meeting Soviet leader Nikita Khrushchev's offer to support wars of national liberation in former colonial areas. Kennedy's advisers developed a concept known as 'flexible response' that called for more measured actions than the 'massive retaliation' of Eisenhower's New Look. The Kennedy team recognized that the United States needed to pay closer attention to the internal political struggles in Vietnam and other developing nations. Crises elsewhere in the world, however, did not allow the new administration time to review recent US policy in Vietnam in terms of Vietnam's history. During his first months in office, Kennedy experienced foreign policy reverses in Cuba and Berlin and felt compelled to accept a compromise in the civil war in Laos. Feeling international and domestic pressure to stand firm somewhere, Kennedy and his top aides decided that Vietnam was the place.

Hence, despite mounting evidence of Diem's liabilities, Kennedy plunged ahead with a belief that American determination would prove sufficient to sustain the Diem experiment.

From Truman and Eisenhower, Kennedy inherited a commitment to assist those Vietnamese threatened by the ideology and control of the DRV. To renege on that commitment would have been, in Kennedy's view, a sign of weakness that would damage the global credibility of the United States to counter Soviet- and Chinese-backed aggression. In April 1961, the poorly disguised US support of the failed Bay of Pigs invasion of Cuba was a major international embarrassment to the administration. In August, the Soviet Union began construction of the Berlin Wall. In his inaugural address the previous January, the president had made a commitment that the United States would 'pay any price, bear any burden, meet any hardship, support any friend, oppose any foe to assure the survival and the success of liberty.'[41] To convince global adversaries and domestic critics that the United States had an answer to the communist-led challenge to Diem's government, the Kennedy team initiated counterinsurgency warfare in South Vietnam.[42]

The administration's counterinsurgency plan contained military, economic, psychological, covert, and financial sections, but the moves to implement the plan marked a clear militarization of US assistance to Diem. Eisenhower's military assistance program had limited the RVN's armed forces to 150,000 and had kept uniformed US military advisers in South Vietnam under 900. In May 1961 Kennedy authorized a personnel ceiling of 200,000 for the South's regular military forces and an expansion of local self-defense forces. Four hundred US Army Special Forces (Green Beret) troops went to the Central Highlands to train Montagnard tribesmen in antiguerrilla warfare. To reassure Diem of continued US support, Kennedy sent Vice President Lyndon Johnson to visit Saigon. The president also directed the Pentagon to examine 'the size and composition of forces which would be desirable in the case of a possible commitment of U.S. forces to Vietnam.'[43]

These demonstrations of American resolve failed to impress the DRV and NLF. During the summer, infiltration along the Ho Chi Minh Trail from the north doubled, although Hanoi still worried about the risk of direct US attacks on the DRV. The Politburo in the northern capital was also aware that the DRV's principal supplier, the Soviet Union, wanted the military conflict kept limited. The NLF continued political work in the form of both propaganda and intimidation among the South Vietnamese, and it organized about 10,000 men and women into the People's Liberation Armed Forces (PLAF). Known by people inside and outside of Vietnam as 'Vietcong,' the PLAF mounted increasing numbers of guerrilla attacks that reached into the vicinity of Saigon itself.[44]

In October the president sent two of his principal White House advisers, Deputy National Security Adviser Walt Rostow and General Maxwell Taylor, to assess the situation. They found the Diem regime suffering from a lack of confidence and recommended a 'limited partnership' between Washington and Saigon to enable the ARVN to take the military initiative against the guerrillas. They urged specifically that an 8000-man US military task force be deployed to Vietnam. Concerned that such a move would greatly increase US risks, high-level State Department officials – Chester Bowles, W. Averell Harriman, and George Ball – favored negotiation with Hanoi. Kennedy rejected both the task force and negotiation. He accepted the idea of a 'limited partnership,' but in his view negotiations would undermine the already tarnished credibility of America's commitment.[45]

On 22 November 1961, Kennedy officially authorized a 'joint effort' that would not only continue but would increase US aid to the RVN. During 1962 the number of US military advisers reached 9000, a tenfold increase over the Eisenhower level.[46] Modern US military technology and equipment, including helicopters and armored personnel carriers, added to the ARVN's mobility and firepower. To provide an effective command structure for this mounting military effort, Washington created the Military Assistance Command, Vietnam (MACV). Annual US economic and military aid to South Vietnam tripled. To combat the insurgency in rural areas, MACV and the RVN constructed about 3000 'strategic hamlets.' These fortified villages were designed to provide security from NLF terror, insulation from communist propaganda, and tangible evidence of Saigon's concern for the agrarian population. This surge in US assistance and innovation in rural security created a facade of progress in the counterinsurgency effort. Washington expressed cautious optimism that the American solution for Vietnam was making headway.

The battle of Ap Bac, southwest of Saigon, dramatically dispelled this image on 2 January 1963. An NLF battalion routed an ARVN force ten times its size. Although the ARVN were equipped with the best American equipment and had tactical air cover, the officers reacted with confusion. Their troops showed little will to fight, reflecting the generally low level of popular support for Diem among the people in the south. Conversely, the NLF fighters gained a great boost of confidence from having downed five helicopters and winning the engagement.

MACV headquarters claimed Ap Bac was an ARVN victory because the enemy withdrew at the end of the day, but journalists and US military advisers who witnessed the fighting knew otherwise.

Another indicator of the frailty of the RVN was the strong resentment of Diem among many of the nation's Buddhists. The usually apolitical Buddhist clergy were challenging the regime's oppression and its favoritism to Catholics, and some monks even burned themselves to death in powerful antigovernment protests. The self-immolations received notoriety throughout the world through graphic newspaper photographs. This 'Buddhist crisis' ended hope among US leaders that Diem could ever create an effective government. American officials, including the president, began to consider a change of leadership in Saigon.[47]

The ire of the Buddhists and of many US officials focused principally on Diem's brother Ngo Dinh Nhu. Nhu directed the regime's secret police activities, including attacks on Buddhist pagodas, which he declared to be dangerous subversive centers. On 24 August 1963, a State Department cable to Ambassador Henry Cabot Lodge in Saigon authorized the ambassador to demand that Diem remove Nhu from the government. This instruction also permitted the embassy to inform dissident South Vietnamese generals that the United States would not interfere with a coup if Diem failed to oust his brother. It was clear that the Kennedy administration was giving up on Diem, but not giving up on finding an American solution for South Vietnam under new leadership.

Despite the 'green light' from Washington, no coup occurred in August or September, and Diem and Nhu defied pressure from Lodge to make changes in the regime. In October, Taylor and Secretary of Defense Robert McNamara met in Saigon with Diem and Nhu and separately with some of the generals. They reported to the president that a coup was unlikely, that some progress was being made in combating the armed insurgency, and that Diem was not going to get rid of Nhu. They recommended increasing pressure on the Saigon government by withholding various types of US assistance, including reducing the number of US advisers in the RVN by 1000. Perhaps Diem could be induced to relax his repressive policies that were fueling dissent. In discussing the report, Kennedy's aides argued over how best to handle Diem. Undecided himself, the president agreed to the increased pressure and authorized the substance of the Taylor-McNamara report as National Security Action Memorandum (NSM) 263 on 11 October.

The US moves to coerce Diem and Nhu and the 'green light' from August prompted the generals to resume scheming. Aware of talk of a coup, the US embassy did not interfere. The plotters seized power in Saigon on 1 November 1963, and after an attempt to escape, Diem and Nhu were murdered by soldiers sent to put them under arrest. There is no evidence that US leaders desired or anticipated the killing of the brothers, but Washington was not surprised by the coup itself.[48]

Kennedy's assassination on 22 November made it forever impossible to know how he would have dealt with the South Vietnamese leaders who succeeded Diem. Some Kennedy aides later argued that his persistent doubts about the American course in Vietnam would have led him, if reelected in 1964, to have withdrawn the United States from the conflict and avoided the massive escalation that occurred in 1965. They note, for example, the anticipated 1000-man reduction in US personnel mentioned in NSM 263.[49] There is other evidence that Kennedy had a plan for US withdrawal from Vietnam that was known only to a few close advisers. His actual decisions from January 1961 to November 1963, however, give Kennedy significant responsibility for further Americanizing and militarizing the South Vietnamese government's battle with the North Vietnamese and NLF. NSM 263 did not reduce, but reaffirmed the US commitment to defeat of the NLF insurgency.

As long as he lived, Kennedy maintained that the security of South Vietnam was vitally important to the security of the United States. In a September 1963 television interview, the president acknowledged that some Americans did not like the Saigon government and had recommended a withdrawal of US support from the RVN. 'That only makes it easy for the Communists,' he reasoned; 'I think we should stay.'[50] He never expressed doubt that the United States could somehow carry through on its commitment to the survival of South Vietnam. When Kennedy died, over 16,000 American military advisers were in the RVN, and over 100 Americans had been killed in action there in the thousand days since he had pledged in his inaugural address that the United States would 'pay any price' in the defense of liberty. Diem's failure to gain a popular following had frustrated the American goal to build a non-communist nation around him, but when Diem and Kennedy were murdered in 1963, there had been no official American reassessment of the strategic value of South Vietnam.[51] The commitment, in fact, was stronger than ever.

3

Credibility: Lyndon Johnson's War

On 22 November 1963, Lyndon Baines Johnson came suddenly and unexpectedly into the presidency of the United States. In the two years that followed, he made a series of decisions that escalated US involvement in Vietnam into a major war with the DRV, and then he continued to expand the size of that American military intervention for two more years. The Vietnam War became the American war in Vietnam, and it became Lyndon Johnson's war. Both ambitious and visionary, Johnson had always pursued political power, but he had never wanted to be a war president. His public passion was the domestic reform agenda of the liberal Democrats begun in the days of Franklin Roosevelt's New Deal. His dream was to create a 'Great Society' in America that would ensure a basic level of well-being for all citizens. During the Second World War he also shared Roosevelt's internationalism, and after the war as a leader in Congress he supported the role of the United States as the champion of the global fight against tyranny and communism. He had a powerful faith in American ability at home and abroad to improve the condition of mankind. After he entered the White House, he told his national security adviser McGeorge Bundy: 'What I really think our role in the world is is ... to have enough power to prevent weak people from being gobbled up and then sharing what we have to prevent people from dying at forty with disease and starving to death and growing up in ignorance. ... I am trying to do it at home. I would like to do it abroad.'[1]

For Johnson, the commitment to sustain South Vietnam that was undertaken by Truman and renewed by Eisenhower and Kennedy continued in full force. For the leaders of the Democratic Republic of Vietnam (DRV), their commitment to national liberation was also unwavering. Washington and Hanoi became determined adversaries that by 1967 were locked in stalemate. To preserve their own internal and international credibility, the leadership of both sides chose to continue fighting rather than

41

to compromise. The credibility of US purpose and global power was at stake, but so too was the credibility of the Johnson administration with the American public. Disdainfully referring to North Vietnam as a 'raggedy ass little fourth rate country,' Johnson could not conceive that Hanoi could thwart Washington's ability to impose an American solution in Vietnam.[2] Eventually US determination would, in his view, overwhelm the communists' bogus promises of national liberation. As the magnitude and cost of this task grew under Johnson's leadership, however, Americans began to doubt their president's word. Citizens increasingly questioned whether the administration was honestly portraying the progress and prospects of the war. By the time Johnson left office, his domestic credibility was as tattered as America's international image.

To the Gulf of Tonkin

Johnson was virtually obsessed with the credibility of the US commitment to South Vietnam from the outset of his administration. Following the coup against Diem, the leadership of the Republic of Vietnam (RVN) was in the hands of an uninspiring military committee headed by Duong Van (Big) Minh. Even before Kennedy's funeral, Johnson was insisting to White House aides that South Vietnam could not be allowed to 'go under.' He did not want the 'fellas' in Moscow and Beijing to 'think we're yellow and we don't mean what we say.'[3] A perception of weakness could encourage Soviet or Chinese aggression, in his view. Four days after Kennedy's murder, Johnson approved National Security Action Memorandum No. 273 that restated, in language very similar to the Truman Doctrine, the US pledge to assist the South Vietnamese 'to win their contest against the externally directed and supported communist conspiracy.'[4] Drafted by the NSC before Kennedy's death, this document placed Johnson's policies firmly in the containment tradition. Determined not to lose Vietnam as Truman had been accused of losing China, Johnson instructed Ambassador Henry Cabot Lodge to give the leaders in Saigon his personal promise that the United States 'intends to stand by our word.'[5]

In large measure it was Johnson's fear of negative consequences that propelled his sense of commitment and his concern with credibility. The new president had an intimidating and overbearing personality that masked his personal and political insecurity. He worried especially about the shadow of the fallen president over his domestic leadership.

He later told a biographer that he had nightmares of Robert Kennedy, the slain president's brother, accusing him of cowardice, of betraying South Vietnam, and of letting 'a democracy fall into the hands of the Communists.'[6] Johnson knew his own strength was in domestic politics and not international and military affairs. He was overawed by the expertise of the military brass and of what he called the 'Harvards' in the foreign policy establishment. Beyond his personal fear of failure was his overarching passion for domestic reform. He worried that his dream of a Great Society within America would founder if the nation turned its attention to a major war in Asia. Ironically, it was this preoccupation with the consequences of a large war – whether successful or unsuccessful – that led him into the combat he preferred to avoid.[7]

Johnson wanted only a limited war, and he constantly asked his advisers how much US military aid was enough. Invariably they recommended increases because conditions within South Vietnam continued to deteriorate. By the spring of 1964, vast areas of South Vietnam were under National Liberation Front (NLF) control and the infiltration of men and matériel from the North had grown. The strategic hamlets had largely ceased to function due to corrupt management by the RVN and peasant resistance to being moved from ancestral homes to remote locations. Simply assisting the South against the North was not enough. In June, Johnson sent one of America's most accomplished combat officers to head MACV – General William C. Westmoreland. The new commander was unimpressed by pacification schemes like the strategic hamlets. He immediately requested more American military personnel to help the Army of the Republic of Vietnam (ARVN), and Washington allowed the US Army advisory strength to surpass 23,000.

While MACV's (Military Assistance Command, Vietnam) size increased in the South, Johnson's White House aides turned their attention to the North. Not only was counterinsurgency warfare not working well in the South, but Secretary of Defense Robert McNamara, Secretary of State Dean Rusk, Walt Rostow, and other senior aides whom Johnson had retained from Kennedy's administration were convinced that Hanoi, not the NLF, was the true enemy. Pressure on the North, they reasoned, would strengthen the South, but such coercion had to be covert because the United States could not assault the DRV without provocation. Through the spring and summer of 1964, the United States secretly gathered intelligence, spread propaganda, and supported an increase in South Vietnamese commando raids on the coast of North Vietnam as part of a covert operation codenamed OPLAN 34A. Seemingly unimpressed by this harassment, Hanoi stepped up its aid to the NLF, and the Pentagon began to prepare contingency plans for air strikes against North Vietnam as a possible next step.[8]

The pretext that Johnson needed to launch selective bombing of the North came in early August. On 2 August, Vietnamese torpedo boats engaged the *USS Maddox*, a destroyer, in the area of the Gulf of Tonkin where the OPLAN 34A raids had been occurring. The *Maddox* and US carrier-based aircraft repulsed the torpedo boats. On the night of 4 August under poor weather conditions, the *Maddox* and the destroyer *USS Turner Joy* reported another North Vietnamese attack. The Joint Chiefs of Staff (JCS) immediately urged Johnson to launch retaliatory air strikes against DRV naval facilities. Follow-up reports from the gulf cautioned, however, that poor visibility and other factors raised doubts that a second attack had occurred. After reviewing many messages, Admiral U. S. Grant Sharp, commander in chief of US Pacific forces, concluded that 'no doubt now existed that an attack on the destroyers had been carried out.'[9] With that assurance, the president ordered the bombing of North Vietnamese coastal bases at Vinh. Because of the confusion about the facts of the 4 August attack, charges circulated long afterward that Johnson had used a false report of an attack to justify the air raids. It is probably true that there was no attack and there was no doubt that the White House welcomed an opportunity to punish North Vietnam. It is also evident, however, that Johnson thought the attack was verified.[10]

The president may have believed that he had a real incident, but he was still guilty of a serious deception. Without revealing OPLAN 34A, Johnson informed Congress that Hanoi was guilty of unprovoked attacks on US ships on the high seas. As commander in chief, he had ordered the raids at Vinh, but he then sought and obtained a congressional resolution authorizing 'all necessary measures to repel any armed attacks against the forces of the United States and to prevent further armed aggression.'[11] This Tonkin Gulf Resolution passed the House of Representatives unanimously and the Senate with only two dissenting votes and became the principal legal authority for the massive American war effort that subsequently emerged in Vietnam. In August 1964, however, Johnson wanted to keep the war limited. He calculated mistakenly that the near unanimous vote in Congress and the bombing of North Vietnamese territory would be enough to deter the DRV from its support of southern insurgency. He judged correctly that his firm but measured response to the Tonkin Gulf naval incidents would help him in his impending presidential contest with Republican candidate Barry Goldwater, who advocated widening the war. In the November 1964 election, Johnson won in a landslide. The near unanimous vote for the Gulf of Tonkin Resolution and Johnson's decisive electoral victory revealed solid political support for the president's moves in Vietnam. He had gained these successes at the expense of candor, however, and the deception would lead to loss of credibility later.

Americanization of the War

In South Vietnam the demonstrations of American determination did not improve the Saigon government's prospects. In fact, the DRV and NLF interpreted the US actions as preliminary to expanded fighting and accelerated their military preparations in the South. Political instability mounted as Buddhists and Catholics continued to clash and various civilian and military leaders in Saigon jockeyed for power. Having crossed the bombing threshold in August, a majority of Johnson's inner circle recommended the use of more American air power. Under-Secretary of State George Ball pointed out that bombing the North did not directly pressure the insurgents in the South, and he also warned that a major air campaign could force China, the USSR, or both to intervene directly to rescue their socialist allies in Hanoi. Most of the president's aides believed, however, that bombing should be tried to bolster Southern morale, to slow infiltration, and to intimidate the North and its allies. With regard to possible reaction by the Soviets and Chinese, there was also risk if the United States did nothing. The USSR had new leaders and the People's Republic of China (PRC) had new nuclear weapons. A collapse in Saigon at this juncture could have encouraged Moscow and Beijing to challenge the United States elsewhere in the world. As a result of these discussions within the administration, in December 1964 Johnson approved a top secret plan that included the bombing of North Vietnam and the likelihood of sending US ground forces to South Vietnam.[12]

The president did not rush to implement this more aggressive policy. During the election campaign he had pledged restraint in Vietnam, and it would have been politically unwise to renege immediately on that promise. The internal political structure in the RVN remained very unstable. The US embassy in Saigon was trying to urge the various factions in Saigon to get together well enough for the US to have something to save. In the first half of 1965 Johnson made a series of fateful decisions to Americanize completely the combat against the DRV and its Southern allies in the NLF. This Americanization took two forms: (1) a sustained and gradually increasing US air bombardment of targets in South and North Vietnam; and (2) the deployment to South Vietnam of entire US combat divisions with supporting elements. These moves began a three-year escalation that reached prodigious proportions. US bombing tonnage eventually exceeded levels in the Second World War, and US troops in South Vietnam surpassed the half-million mark in 1968.

The air war began in February 1965. A Vietcong attack on the American advisers' base at Pleiku provided a reason for a retaliatory air strike. Within 48 hours Washington ordered 'sustained reprisal' bombing. Code named ROLLING THUNDER, this bombing campaign became a regular and expanding feature of the American war in Vietnam. US fighter-bombers from bases in Thailand and from aircraft carriers in the Gulf of Tonkin and the South China Sea attacked military bases, supply depots, and infiltration routes in North and South Vietnam. During the first year of ROLLING THUNDER, there were 25,000 sorties flown against North Vietnam. In 1966 the number was 79,000, and in 1967 it reached 108,000 sorties delivering almost 250,000 tons of explosives. The target lists expanded from strictly military targets to include farms, factories, and transportation lines in North Vietnam and the Ho Chi Minh Trail supply route in Laos.[13]

From the beginning of the bombing, American strategists debated the effectiveness of air power in defeating a political insurgency in a predominantly agricultural country. Despite the American bombs, dollars, and military advisers, the Vietcong continued to inflict heavy casualties on the ARVN, and the political situation in Saigon grew worse. In March 1965, two battalions of US Marines landed at Danang to protect the US air base there. By June 1965, there had been five governments in the South since Diem's death, and the newest regime headed by General Nguyen Van Thieu and Air Marshall Nguyen Cao Ky inspired little confidence. Assistant Secretary of State William Bundy lamented that the Thieu-Ky government was 'absolutely the bottom of the barrel.'[14] To hold off defeat, the JCS endorsed Westmoreland's request for 150,000 US troops to take the ground offensive in the South. The Pentagon clearly wanted control of the ground war.

Johnson well understood the gravity of such action and from 21 to 28 July wrestled with his decision. He sought advice from several sources, but not from the Saigon government itself. In the words of South Vietnamese diplomat Bui Diem, the 'unself-conscious arrogance of the American approach' was 'appalling.'[15] All of Johnson's senior advisers except Ball favored meeting Westmoreland's request. With remarkable insight, Ball warned of a credibility trap. With the deployment of ground troops, he predicted, 'our involvement will be so great that we cannot – without national humiliation – stop short of achieving our complete objectives.'[16] McNamara, on the other hand, assured the president that if the United States were to 'expand substantially the US military pressure' and 'launch a vigorous effort' at negotiations, this program would likely 'bring about a favorable solution to the Vietnam problem.'[17]

Johnson decided to commit the forces that the Pentagon had requested. To order US troops to wage a ground war and to continue the massive aerial campaign in Vietnam was not what the president desired. He later lamented to close aides that 'I want war like I want polio, [but] what you want and what your image is are two different things.'[18] To his wife he confided: 'I can't get out. I can't finish with what I've got. So what the hell do I do?'[19] Despite the anguish, Johnson believed he had no choice but to authorize the greater use of military force. He judged that any compromise diplomatic settlement would be a political victory for Hanoi. In his memoirs he recorded that 'a political collapse in Saigon' would lead to 'an ignominious American withdrawal' from Southeast Asia and leave the entire region 'ripe for plucking.'[20] Considerations of global strategy and ideology made any appearance of surrender to an ally of Moscow and Beijing unacceptable.

On 28 July, Johnson made a purposefully understated announcement at a midday press conference that 50,000 US troops would go to South Vietnam immediately and that additional forces would follow. By the end of the year, there would be 184,300 US personnel in the South. In his public statement the president described North Vietnam as waging overt military aggression against South Vietnam. 'We did not choose to be the guardians at the gate,' he explained, 'but there is no one else.'[21] He had made the Vietnam War the American war in Vietnam, but he did not declare it a war. His Great Society legislation was at that moment approaching final passage in Congress. He was preparing for what he termed a 'war on poverty' at home, and he was not going to divert public attention from it. As with the Gulf of Tonkin Resolution, Johnson was being less than candid – not a way to build credibility.

American strategy

The Vietnam War began without fanfare in the United States, and it was from the outset a very different kind of war than the conflicts in recent American memory. For Americans, the Second World War had begun with the shocking Japanese surprise attack on US territory at Pearl Harbor, and President Franklin Roosevelt had captured the public's anger and determination with a rousing speech to Congress declaring war with Japan. The Korean War began for the United States with no formal declaration, but President Harry Truman's order sending US forces into battle in Korea was consistent with Washington's announced containment policy. It seemed to be logical, even obligatory, for the United States to respond with force to communist-led North Korea's conventional military assault against America's ally South Korea. The Vietnam War, however, was not a war of aggression but of insurgency. It was not a contest for territory with progress marked by lines on a map. It was an attempt by military force to provide security and legitimacy for a particular political group in Vietnam. Knowing who in Vietnam was America's enemy was difficult, since there were no fixed battle lines and the enemy often wore, not uniforms, but the black peasant clothing of the farmers the United States said it was defending. Setting military objectives and measuring progress in this context was a frustration throughout the conflict.

The United States had crossed the line from aiding and advising the South Vietnamese military to actually fighting the war against the DRV and NLF, but Johnson had made the political decision that it would be a limited war. He rejected recommendations by the JCS that he mobilize the reserves and National Guard and resisted McNamara's proposal for levying war taxes. The president knew that such steps would require congressional authorization. He understood Capitol Hill well and predicted that conservative members of Congress would use such military mobilization bills as a means to postpone his liberal Great Society program. The 20 billion dollar annual expenditure on the war came from deficit financing with its inevitable inflationary effect. To meet manpower needs, the administration relied on existing authority to use the military draft.

Military conscription in the United States operated through the Selective Service System in much the same manner as it had during and since the Second World War. Men over the age of 18 were subject to the draft, but not all were needed to serve, even when draft calls doubled and went to 35,000 per month with the deployment of US troops to Vietnam. Men could be exempted completely or deferred from induction through a variety of classifications based upon health, occupation, educational status, or hardship. The number of draftees inducted in 1965 was 106,000, and that total rose to 339,000 in 1966. Over half of those drafted served in Vietnam. Because being drafted meant highly increased risk of exposure to combat, the fairness of the selection process began to come under scrutiny.[22]

Only about 10 percent of the men who reached the age of 18 during the war served in Vietnam. They numbered about two and a half million, and not all were draftees. Many enlisted voluntarily, although the existence of the draft helped induce enlistments. Because the administration was avoiding full mobilization, there were no national enlistment drives. Statistically, the draftees in Vietnam were poorer and less educated than the averages for their age group. In part the explanation was that selective service rules allowed deferments for men in college, who were mostly middle class and above. Another statistic from the first year of the war revealed that 20 percent of the combat casualties were African Americans, although that racial group comprised only 13 percent of all military personnel. Many of these men had joined the military as a career opportunity and chose combat specialties to receive higher pay. They comprised much of the first wave of soldiers deployed before the draft increases began affecting the staffing of units. In later years of the war the profile of casualties by race began to approximate the overall racial percentages of young Americans. Throughout the war, though, information on income and education indicated that about 80 percent of the US soldiers in Vietnam were from poor or working-class backgrounds. General Westmoreland himself referred to it as a blue-collar war.

Johnson did not relish sending young men to war. Even as it stepped up military escalation, his administration professed readiness to negotiate a settlement with Hanoi. The president announced in a speech at Johns Hopkins University on 7 April 1965 that the United States would enter into 'unconditional discussions' and offered an incentive of a billion-dollar economic development project for the Mekong River Valley similar to America's famous Tennessee Valley Authority (TVA).[23] In part this speech was a gesture calculated to counter domestic criticism that the bombing campaign had not given enough opportunity for a diplomatic solution. For Johnson, however, the Mekong TVA proposal was also sincere, if naive. It fit his political deal-making experience and his desire to help people. 'Old Ho can't turn me down,' he assured his press secretary, but indeed the DRV leaders dismissed the billion dollars as a 'bribe.'[24] In May the United States conducted a brief bombing pause as another gesture to begin talks, but Hanoi labeled it a 'worn out trick.'[25]

As long as Johnson remained president, combat not compromise was the reality. Neither the United States nor the DRV would take a meaningful first step toward real negotiations. Having been frustrated by compromise at the Geneva Conference of 1954, the Politburo absolutely rejected the legitimacy of the RVN and of the US presence in the South. Northern negotiators insisted that no talks were possible as long as US forces were in Vietnam. Conversely, Washington declared that the DRV and its NLF agents were conducting a war of aggression against the South. The United States would not remove its troops until Hanoi ceased infiltration of the South and recognized the existence of the Saigon government. Both sides chose to accept armed conflict rather than to retreat from their basic positions.[26]

While US planes bombed targets in North Vietnam, Westmoreland went on the offensive against the Southern insurgents. The general formed his battle plan within the doctrine of limited warfare, which meant gradual escalation of bombing and incremental troop deployments. Politically, the president did not want the war to intrude on American domestic life. Internationally, the risks of a wider war with China and the Soviet Union meant that the United States would not go all out to annihilate North Vietnam. Thus Westmoreland chose a strategy of attrition in the South, that is, inflicting heavier losses on the enemy than Hanoi could replace. Using air mobility and massive firepower, the MACV commander intended to exhaust the enemy while limiting US casualties.[27]

Responding to the American escalation, Hanoi deployed into the South units of the People's Army of Vietnam (PAVN), which was the regular North Vietnamese Army (NVA). In October, General Vo Nguyen Giap, the PAVN commander, launched a major offensive in the Central Highlands, southwest of Pleiku. Westmoreland responded with the 1st Air Cavalry Division. Through much of November, in the battle of the Ia Drang Valley, US and North Vietnamese forces engaged in heavy combat for the first time. Westmoreland used helicopters extensively for troop movements, resupply, medical evacuation, and tactical air support. US Air Force tactical bombers and even huge B-52 strategic bombers attacked enemy positions. The Americans ultimately forced the NVA out of the valley and killed ten times as many enemy soldiers as they lost. The battle convinced Westmoreland that search and destroy tactics using air mobility would work in accomplishing the attrition strategy. Yet, soon after the PAVN departed, so too did the air cavalry. Clearly, control of territory was not the US military objective.[28]

The goal of the attrition strategy was to weaken the fighting strength of the PAVN and People's Liberation Armed Forces (PLAF). In an effort to track the effectiveness of this strategy, the Pentagon devised a host of statistical measurements of the war's progress. Secretary McNamara was a former president of Ford Motor Company and had a high degree of faith in the quantitative management methods of systems analysis. Careful records were kept on numbers of combat aircraft sorties, artillery shells expended, and basically anything that could be counted. The one such item that came to symbolize and even to dominate this accounting process was 'body count' – that is, the actual or estimated number of enemy combatants killed. Although counting enemy dead seemed to be the ultimate measure of attrition, it was in fact a very poor yardstick. Since the counting was done by the troops at battle sites without other witnesses, it could easily be inflated, especially when commanders rewarded individuals or units with promotions and extra leave for high body counts. A worse result was when units achieved high body counts using their own rule that 'if it's dead and Vietnamese, it's VC,' which meant that noncombatants including women and children, especially in rural villages, became targets. Such assaults from American air and ground forces in the South did little to win political adherents for Saigon.

Westmoreland had what he believed was a workable strategy with a limited number of troops, but he repeatedly asked for more. Although he had avoided sending US combat forces to Vietnam, former president Eisenhower confidentially advised Johnson that he 'should sweep the enemy with overwhelming force' and not take 'piddling steps.'[29] Johnson continued to worry, however, about the reaction of congressional conservatives to a dramatic increase in the war effort. Work on the Department of Defense budget for the next fiscal year indicated that even at present levels the war would push total defense expenditures over $110 billion. Johnson instructed McNamara not to submit a figure of over $57 billion to the House Appropriations Committee because the legislators, seeking to avoid new taxes, would then eliminate the poverty programs to pay for the war. McNamara concurred that there was a risk 'your Great Society is going to be gutted.' In yet another misrepresentation to Congress, Johnson connived with McNamara to 'put off a decision on extra troops until February–March,' that is, until after the budget had been approved.[30]

As Johnson maneuvered to keep the congressional right-wing at bay, he also sought to deflect criticism from liberal critics in Congress and from *New York Times* editorial writers, who were calling for a bombing pause to encourage negotiations. He agreed to allow a brief holiday cease-fire during Christmas 1965 to continue into the new year, although he believed that 'the odds are 95 to 5 that nothing will happen' on the diplomatic front. He had the Department of State consult with the governments in Britain and Poland, which had previously offered to be diplomatic go-betweens, but basically he was trying to gain public support for continued bombing by demonstrating that 'we have gone the last mile' to invite talks. Responsible for direction of the air campaign against North Vietnam, Admiral Sharp grew restive with the pause, complaining to the JCS that his forces were being 'required to fight the war with one hand tied behind their backs,' and recommended immediate resumption of ROLLING THUNDER.[31] On 31 January Johnson authorized renewed bombing of North Vietnam, and by 30 June US troop levels in South Vietnam stood at 267,500.

Stalemate

The Americanization of the war was helping the Saigon government survive, but after a year of heavy US intervention there was little other evidence of success or even a definition of what might be termed victory. Twice in 1966, in February at Honolulu and in October at Manila, Johnson held personal meetings with President Nguyen Van Thieu and Premier Nguyen Cao Ky of South Vietnam. In the first meeting he pressed the RVN leaders and his own senior commanders for results, and in the fall conference he sought assurances of progress. The mood at both meetings was positive, and, at the president's prompting, Westmoreland even declared in October that there was 'light at the end of the tunnel.' Throughout 1966 the gradual US build-up in South Vietnam continued in keeping with Johnson's 'enough but not too much' formula. The US force level reached 385,000 at the end of the year, with seven US combat divisions and other specialized units in the RVN. With American aid, the ARVN expanded to 11 divisions. While Westmoreland prepared for future large-unit search and destroy operations, Army and Marine units conducted smaller operations. Although the 'body count' mounted, attrition was not changing the political equation in South Vietnam. The NLF continued to exercise more effective control in many areas than did the government.[32] The bombing campaign was not slowing infiltration. Noting these trends, McNamara questioned Westmoreland's optimistic assessments and concluded that the war could drag on much longer. Although he maintained a public facade of confidence, the defense secretary privately advised the president to seek negotiations with Hanoi.

Johnson remained skeptical of the DRV's willingness to talk, but in

November a possible diplomatic arrangement, code named MARIGOLD, presented itself. Responding to a Polish offer to help start discussions, Washington suggested a two-part plan in which the United States would first suspend bombing of the North and Hanoi would then give private assurances that it had stopped infiltration of the South. The DRV broke off the fragile contact when, after several weeks of inactivity in the air war, the United States conducted an air strike near Hanoi on 2 December. The North Vietnamese accused Washington of negotiating in bad faith, although the bombing lull had been weather related all along and the White House had not connected the pause to the exploratory talks.[33]

Neither side was ready to negotiate in earnest, but both sides continued to probe diplomatic possibilities in January 1967. The State Department attempted to establish contact with North Vietnamese diplomats in Moscow, and less conventionally two American journalists brought back to Washington a report of a private meeting they had in Hanoi with Ho Chi Minh. These moves failed to produce substantive discussions, and on 8 February 1967, Johnson even sent a personal message to Ho suggesting 'direct talks between trusted representatives.' His tone was firm, however. Rather than a phased disengagement as proposed in the MARIGOLD contacts, Johnson insisted that the DRV must stop infiltration of South Vietnam before the United States would promise to stop bombing and increasing the size of its ground forces. Ho replied with equal intensity. He accused the United States of 'aggression' and promised that 'the Vietnamese people will never yield to force nor agree to talks under the menace of bombs.'[34]

In January 1967, Westmoreland was ready to implement his big-unit, attrition strategy for what he believed would be military victory. He assigned the ARVN primarily to occupation, pacification, and security duties in populated areas. This arrangement freed large US combat formations numbering in the tens of thousands to sweep rural areas. Westmoreland set in motion operations CEDAR FALLS and JUNCTION CITY in an area known as the Iron Triangle, north and west of Saigon. US forces inflicted heavy casualties on the enemy and destroyed large amounts of supplies. MACV declared vast areas to be 'free-strike zones,' which meant that US and ARVN artillery and tactical aircraft, as well as B-52 'carpet bombing,' could target anyone or anything in the area. Chemical defoliants sprayed from aircraft laid bare thousands of acres of natural vegetation and food crops in suspected NLF-controlled areas.[35] As journalist Jonathan Schell described the fate of one village in the Iron Triangle, it appeared that the objective was to annihilate 'every possible indication that the village of Ben Suc had ever existed.'[36] The result of the operations was general devastation and camps crowded with hostile refugees, but not the decisive blow Westmoreland had expected. The Vietcong main force units in the Iron Triangle had largely evaded the attacks, and soon after the operation ended the NLF political infrastructure was back in the villages that had not been destroyed.

How were the DRV and the NLF able to survive the tremendous military force of the United States? The bombing of North Vietnam and the Ho Chi Minh Trail had not coerced diplomatic concessions or lowered infiltration of men and supplies into the South. Indications were that air raids on the North stiffened popular determination in a fashion similar to the British public's response to German bombing of England in the Second World War. The destructiveness of bombing in the South provided effective propaganda material about how little the Americans cared about the people. Since most of the PAVN and PLAF units in the South were light infantry that did not require a high volume of supplies, interdicting their supply lines had only limited utility. Although the American air war was ineffective much of the time and even counterproductive, it continued. It appealed to US leaders because it produced fewer American casualties than ground combat, was conducted largely by highly motivated officers not draftees, and held out the hope of providing a simple solution to a complex socio-political conflict.

The attrition strategy in the ground war also collided with a well-conceived DRV counterstrategy that Hanoi termed 'protracted war.' It was essentially the same plan that the Vietminh had used successfully against the French. North Vietnamese strategists avoided large-unit, fixed battles that would allow the Americans to use their technological advantages, and instead PAVN and PLAF units harassed the US and ARVN forces with ambushes, guerrilla raids, booby traps, and mortar and rocket attacks from temporary positions. They assumed that over time the political will of the Americans and the US 'puppet' regime to carry on the fight would weaken. The NLF also created a clandestine political infrastructure in the villages and towns of South Vietnam to recruit followers and gain access to local resources to sustain the armed resistance and to prepare for a general uprising that would topple the RVN government.

Although the theory of protracted war presumed that heroic sacrifice could defeat modern technological warfare, the United States was, in fact, inflicting heavy losses on the enemies of the RVN. The government in Hanoi could claim to be heir to the centuries-old legacy of Vietnamese resistance to outside control and the Vietnamese desire for national unity. Through the Vietminh front it had prevented the return of French colonial rule, and the heroic figure of that struggle, Ho Chi Minh, remained as president of the DRV until his death in 1969. Conversely, the leaders of the RVN – Diem, Thieu, and Ky – regardless of what personal qualities they may have possessed, were stigmatized by an apparent or real dependence on the United States for their political survival. Despite these real advantages enjoyed by the DRV, it was paying a heavy price to contest the RVN.

A significant factor in North Vietnam's ability to stand up to US military power was the aid that the Soviet Union and the People's Republic of China provided to the DRV. The communist nations were not the monolith portrayed by America's Cold War rhetoric, but Moscow and Beijing each had their own reasons for assisting Hanoi. Despite Nikita Khrushchev's flamboyant rhetoric about supporting wars of national liberation, the Soviet Union had taken a cautious approach to the DRV's decision in the early 1960s to support the armed insurrection in South Vietnam. Wary of the independence and nationalism of North Vietnamese leaders, Soviet officials were not eager to risk a confrontation with the United States over Vietnam, but they also knew that to ignore Hanoi's needs would damage their political credibility with other communist states. As the United States escalated its involvement in Indochina, the USSR became the DRV's principal supplier of such vital commodities as industrial and telecommunication equipment, trucks, medical supplies, machine tools, and iron ore. Moscow became especially important to North Vietnam's defense against the American air war. The Soviets provided surface-to-air missiles (SAMs), fighter planes, antiaircraft artillery, radar, and the military advisers to help utilize these modern weapons. Thousands of PAVN officers and soldiers also received training in the Soviet Union. Despite providing this critical assistance, the Kremlin was not able to convince Hanoi of its view that greater restraint and negotiations would be preferable to the dangerous test of strength it was engaged in with the United States.[37]

One of the significant limits to Soviet influence was the complex relationship that the DRV had with China. Despite the long history of Vietnamese wariness of its powerful neighbor, the Chinese communist leadership had a good relationship with key members of the Politburo in Hanoi. Almost immediately after the establishment of the PRC in 1949, China had recognized the DRV as the government of Vietnam and had provided military aid and advice during the war against France. After the Geneva Conference, the PRC did not involve itself directly in Vietnamese affairs, but in the early 1960s Mao Zedong, the chairman of the Chinese Communist Party, took a much publicized interest in the fate of the DRV. On 5 August 1964, the day of the US air attacks in reprisal for the Tonkin Gulf incident, Beijing issued an official statement condemning 'the US imperialist aggression against Vietnam' and declaring 'solidarity with the Vietnamese people.'[38] Mao's motives had a lot to do with his moves to radicalize politics within the PRC and to challenge what he viewed as Moscow's passive support of revolutionary regimes.

In early 1965 as US intervention in Vietnam escalated, the leading members of the DRV Politburo – Ho Chi Minh, Vo Nguyen Giap, Le Duan, Pham Van Dong, and Nguyen Chi Thanh – held personal meetings with their Chinese counterparts – Mao, Premier Zhou Enlai, and General Luo Ruiqing. In these meetings the Chinese indicated that they would send forces to Vietnam if the United States invaded North Vietnam, that they would make clear to the Americans the danger of possible war with China, and that they would try to avoid direct confrontation with US forces but would stand up to them if necessary. They backed up these pledges by sending over 320,000 engineering troops and antiaircraft artillery forces to North Vietnam over the next four years to help defend against air attacks and to rebuild roads and bridges from bomb damage. These Chinese military personnel freed PAVN soldiers for service in the South and kept the DRV supply and communication systems functioning despite the air war.[39] Since Johnson did not believe that Indochina was worth the risk of war with China or the Soviet Union, he consistently refused to authorize any bombing targets or land operations that would have directly engaged the Chinese or Soviet military or logistical operations.

By 1967 it was apparent to Johnson that the US military escalation undertaken in 1965 was costing more and taking longer to get results than had been estimated. Public criticism of his policies and protests against the war were increasing. In February he told his aides that the US war was 'on borrowed time' politically, but he thought that there was still three to one support in the country for strong military action.[40] He noted that the various diplomatic probes had come up with nothing substantial. Westmoreland's effort to strike a decisive blow in the Iron Triangle had also come up empty. In March, the president traveled again to the Pacific to meet with Thieu and Ky. In a conference at Guam, Johnson decided to put emphasis on pacification. He went back to the idea of a Mekong TVA and even brought the former director of the TVA to the meeting. He also named Robert Komer, a civilian member of the White House staff, to head a new pacification operation called Civilian

Operations and Revolutionary Development Support (CORDS). Komer was made a civilian deputy commander of MACV, and CORDS remained a part of US military operations thereafter. It had the task of bringing more social and economic development to rural Vietnamese in an effort to 'win the hearts and minds' of the people. It operated the Chieu Hoi program (that sought to induce defections from the Vietcong), refugee resettlement efforts, public health projects, and other aid programs.[41]

Although the tone at Guam was positive, outside the formal meetings Westmoreland estimated that pacification could take ten more years, and he made yet another request for more troops – 200,000 more – to find and destroy the enemy. The results of CEDAR FALLS and JUNCTION CITY had made McNamara more skeptical than ever about further military escalation, and he sent Johnson a forcefully worded dissent to the general's proposal. 'The war in Vietnam is acquiring a momentum of its own that must be stopped,' he warned. To send more US troops, in his view, 'could lead to a national disaster' and 'would not win the Vietnam war.' 'The enemy has us "stalemated,"' he wrote, and can 'maintain the military "stalemate" by matching our added deployments as necessary.' The secretary of defense advised that US ground operations be kept at existing levels, that bombing of the North be reduced, and that pacification and diplomatic efforts be continued with the goal not being defeat of the DRV and NLF, but 'toward negotiations and toward ending the war on satisfactory terms.' McNamara's final point of his long memorandum was that the war was not enhancing, but was in fact destroying US credibility in the eyes of the world: 'The picture of the world's greatest superpower killing or injuring more than 1,000 noncombatants a month while trying to pound a tiny backward nation into submission on an issue whose merits are hotly disputed is not a pretty one.'[42]

If the war was a standoff, as McNamara asserted, Johnson was not ready to blink. Bolstered by arguments from the JCS in support of Westmoreland's request, the president was determined to keep military pressure on North Vietnam. In a pattern that had become predictable, however, when presented by appeals for more force, Johnson temporized and approved an increase of only 55,000 troops. He did not respond to McNamara's specific criticisms of the effectiveness of MACV's search-and-destroy tactics or the inability of the air war to stop infiltration. There was no general review of the attrition strategy.

With no discernible change in the military and political balance in South Vietnam, McNamara sent another long memorandum to the president on 1 November 1967 that 'addressed fundamental questions that had to be answered.' 'I understood just how hard it would be for the president to consider abandoning the conventional wisdom on Vietnam and changing course,' McNamara wrote in his memoirs, 'but that was what I was recommending.'[43] His specific proposal was a policy he called 'stabilization,' which had three parts: First was 'no increase ... in US forces above the current approved level'; second was 'a bombing halt [that] is likely to lead to talks with Hanoi'; and third were 'programs which involve (a) reduced US casualties, (b) procedures for progressive turn-over to the GVN [Government of South Vietnam] of greater responsibility for security in the South, and (c) lesser destruction of the people and wealth of South Vietnam.'[44]

In a fashion similar to the way he had avoided candid conversation at previous policy junctures, Johnson did not respond directly to McNamara. Instead he shared the memorandum with Secretary of State Rusk and Walt Rostow, his national security adviser. He seemed to be seeking reassurance that the situation did not require the drastic changes McNamara had proposed. He instructed Rostow to avoid divulging the author of the recommendations, but to canvass the opinions of other key aides, such as General Maxwell Taylor, US ambassador to Saigon Ellsworth Bunker, and personal presidential confidants Abe Fortas and Clark Clifford. On 2 November the president met with the Wise Men, an informal group of foreign policy advisors who in the past had generally supported the administration's policies in Vietnam. The group included Taylor, Fortas, Clifford, Ball, McGeorge Bundy, General Omar Bradley, Henry Cabot Lodge, Dean Acheson, and other former high-level officials, as well as McNamara, Rusk, CIA Director Richard Helms, Assistant Secretary of State William Bundy, and other current officials.

The president began the meeting by asking the Wise Men 'if our course in Vietnam was right. If not, how should it be modified?' He noted particular concern about what appeared to be 'deterioration of public support and lack of editorial support for our policies.' Having already received positive military and intelligence briefings, those assembled readily asserted approval. The war was 'an enormous success' in Clifford's view, and he believed that, if the United States kept the pressure on, 'the will of the Viet Cong and the North Vietnamese will wear down.' The president himself summarized that 'generally everyone agrees with our present course in the South.' With regard to public support, Rostow added that 'there are ways of guiding the press to show light at the end of the tunnel.'[45]

This meeting revealed some major inabilities of the Johnson White House to deal honestly with the status of the war. During the meeting the president never called on the secretary of defense to give an estimate of the war's progress. At one point he praised McNamara for his service to the nation and at another time asked him a specific technical question. He never mentioned the secretary's memorandum, and McNamara later wrote that 'the Wise Men had no clue that all this was going on.'[46] In addition, what McNamara may not have known was that Rostow had distorted the intelligence information made available for White House briefings. He had, for example, gone to senior CIA Vietnam analyst George Allen and asked for an intelligence summary that would convince 'congressmen and other White House visitors in the coming weeks that the pacification effort was on track.' Such a report would not have been objective in Allen's view, and he declined 'to be a party to "cooking the books" in the manner he was suggesting.'[47] Rostow eventually got the type of report he desired from another CIA office.

Under mounting public pressure to show results, Johnson ordered Westmoreland to Washington in November 1967 to give a progress report. The general dutifully announced that, although much fighting remained, a cross-over point had arrived in the war of attrition, that is, the losses to the NVA and Vietcong were greater than they could replace. He told a group at the Pentagon that 'the ranks of the Vietcong are thinning steadily,' and he publicly asserted that 'we have reached an important point when the end begins to come into view.'[48] This assessment was debatable. Although NVA and Vietcong losses were three times those of the US and ARVN forces from 1965 to 1967, enemy force levels in the South had actually increased. There was considerable evidence also that the so-called other war for political support in South Vietnam was not going well. Corruption, factionalism, and continued Buddhist protests plagued the Thieu-Ky government. Despite incredible losses, the NLF still controlled many areas. Diplomatic compromises proposed by third countries such as Poland and Great Britain met firm resistance from both Washington and Hanoi. The war indeed was at a stalemate, as McNamara had tried to make Johnson understand. By the end of 1967 there were 485,000 US troops in Vietnam. The escalation had increased the costs of the war in lives and money, but failed to diminish the North's threat to the South.[49]

Since the war was not going as well as the administration's public assurances made it sound, Johnson was exposing his cherished credibility to great risk. The president himself, however, seemed unaware of it. In December 1967 he signed a secret memorandum for the record based upon Rostow's compilation of the responses to McNamara's memorandum, the 'full discussion' at the 2 November meeting, and conversations

with Westmoreland and Bunker. In this document he rejected the 'stabilization' policy and the idea of 'a unilateral and unrequited bombing
stand-down.'[50] As 1967 ended, Johnson gave no public or private indication that he was contemplating any change in strategy or objectives in
the Vietnam War.

4

Contention: Antiwar Protests, the Tet Offensive, and a Tumultuous Election

The US war in Vietnam reached a turning point in 1968. As the level of fighting and the human and financial costs escalated from 1965 to 1968, public opinion in the United States, which at first supported the war, began to change, and a significant and highly vocal protest movement appeared. Organized resistance to the war expanded as the US involvement grew. Lyndon Johnson's efforts in late 1967 to assure the public of progress in the war effort were a direct response to the outspoken criticism of American policy in Vietnam. Only a month after General William Westmoreland, at Johnson's urging, had reported that the end of the war was coming into sight, the military forces of the National Liberation Front (NLF) and the Democratic Republic of Vietnam (DRV) launched a surprise offensive throughout South Vietnam. This Tet Offensive, named for the Vietnamese lunar new year celebration, had a dramatic impact on American public opinion and challenged the credibility of the administration's optimistic forecasts. Although US and Army of the Republic of Vietnam (ARVN) forces reversed the military thrust of the Tet Offensive, the intense fighting began a chain of events that represented a halt in the escalation of the American war. Heavy ground combat continued, but shortly after Tet Johnson reduced the extent of bombing in North Vietnam and withdrew himself as a candidate for reelection. The war figured significantly in the 1968 presidential campaign, although civil rights, law and order, and the national economy were also key issues. Antiwar protests produced a tumultuous and violent Democratic National Convention in Chicago in August. The election in November failed to be a referendum on the war, but it resulted in a very close victory by Republican Richard Nixon over

Johnson's Vice President, Hubert Humphrey. The military and political developments of 1968 had produced a change in American leadership and begun active pursuit of a way for the United States to withdraw with honor, as Nixon put it, from the war.

Antiwar movement

The protest movement in the United States against the Vietnam War had no single organization or source. It was basically a spontaneous and *ad hoc* collection of various pacifists, ideological anti-imperialists, and peace liberals acting individually or in separate groups. It eventually came to include thousands of people engaged in various activities, including political campaigns, petition drives, lobbying of legislators, street demonstrations, draft resistance, and occasionally overt acts of violence. Many in the movement were young and many were students, but the movement also included veteran political activists, ministers, mothers, and even some Vietnam veterans. What direct impact these protests had on official US government policies is difficult to say, especially since the participants lacked coordination and agreement on what they wanted the government to do. Liberals tended to favor a negotiated settlement, and radicals argued for unilateral withdrawal and leaving any settlement to the Vietnamese alone. Although they denied being influenced by the antiwar movement, national leaders were well aware of its existence and tried in various ways to quiet it.

Divisions among Americans over war and peace issues were not new, and antiwar organizations predated the US escalation in Vietnam. Religious pacifists such as Quakers and groups like the Fellowship for Reconciliation, the War Resisters League, and the Women's International League for Peace and Freedom had a long history dating back to the era of the First World War and before. These groups supported conscientious objection and nonviolent civil disobedience against government actions. The advent of the nuclear arms race in the 1950s had led to the creation of the Women Strike for Peace (WSP) and the National Committee for a Sane Nuclear Policy (SANE), which included among its members the famous pediatrician Dr Benjamin Spock. During the early sixties, a group calling itself Students for a Democratic Society (SDS) appeared on college campuses. At its inception at the University of Michigan and elsewhere, SDS was not an anti-war organization. Terming their views 'New Left' to distinguish them from old-line Marxist ideology, the students declared their opposition to big business, big government, and big universities, which they collectively referred to as the Establishment. Although most Americans were not paying a great deal of attention to the possible implications of the growing US involvement with South Vietnam in the 1950s and early 1960s, a few individual members of these existing organizations did voice some concerns. It was also these groups that mounted the first organized protests in 1965 when the Johnson administration began ROLLING THUNDER and then deployed the first US combat divisions to Vietnam.

The bombing campaign prompted Dr Spock, who had endorsed Johnson during the 1964 election campaign, to issue several forceful public letters in protest. On 16 March 1965, an 82-year-old member of WSP, Alice Herz, burned herself to death in Detroit in imitation of the Buddhist acts of resistance in Vietnam. Her dramatic act received little media coverage, but a few days later professors at the University of Michigan staged what they called a 'teach-in' to draw student and public attention to war issues. This tactic of a marathon of lectures and discussions spread to about 100 other campuses, and a teach-in at the University of California at Berkeley with prominent participants such as Spock, folk singer Phil Ochs, and novelist Norman Mailer attracted 20,000 people over a two-day period. The SDS organized a public protest in Washington, DC, on 17 April that attracted about 20,000 people, and the organization also demonstrated against the war at the Oakland, California port where US troops departed for Vietnam.

In the fall after the escalation of US forces began, further protests were organized. On 16 October 1965, a colorful mass of 20,000 mostly young and radical marchers conducted a 25-block parade in Manhattan that also attracted a smaller number of counter-demonstrators denouncing the young people as unpatriotic communists. Not so easy to label, however, was a gathering of about 35,000 mostly well-behaved adults organized by SANE in Washington on 27 November in which speakers called for negotiations. The New York 'happening' attracted more press coverage than the more conventional Washington rally. This difference represented a problem that the antiwar movement had throughout the war. In the minds of many citizens, it acquired an image as a radical fringe element, when in fact many active protesters of the war were essentially mainstream Americans. In November there were also two more self-immolations, one of them outside the Pentagon and visible from McNamara's office window. Although inspiring to antiwar activists, these dramatic events were generally perceived by the public as the acts of fanatics.[1]

Lacking a centralized organization, the antiwar effort during 1966 grew slowly as a grassroots movement of local rallies, petition drives, draft resistance, and small meetings. Although outspoken opposition to the Johnson administration's policy in Southeast Asia remained a minority sentiment, the war's critics began to receive some significant help. In January 1966 a national interfaith group of clergymen – led by Rabbi Abraham Heschel, Lutheran minister Richard Neuhaus, and Jesuit priest Daniel Berrigan – created Clergy and Laymen Concerned about the War in Vietnam (CALCAV), which called for negotiations. In February Senator J. William Fulbright, a liberal Democrat and political ally of Johnson who had come to question the decision to escalate the war, chaired televised Senate hearings that exposed Secretary of State Rusk to tough questioning. They also provided a forum for reputable critics of the war such as George Kennan, the former State Department official who first articulated the idea of containment. Kennan declared that Vietnam was of no strategic value to the United States. The hearings did not alter US policy, but they made dissent more legitimate. Antiwar sentiment failed to strike a responsive chord in the congressional election campaigns of 1966, however, and, in fact, Vietnam was often not even debated by candidates. Domestic issues such as civil rights and the costs of the Great Society antipoverty programs concerned voters more than the war.[2]

In 1967, public opinion polls began to show rising dissatisfaction with the war, and several key developments occurred in the antiwar movement. Polling data at the end of 1967 indicated that 45 percent of Americans thought military intervention had been a mistake, but only 10 percent favored immediate withdrawal. In fact some who wanted the United States out of Vietnam favored a major escalation of US forces to coerce Hanoi into a negotiated settlement. A significant reason for the impatience of Americans was the grim reality that 16,000 of their fellow citizens had died fighting this war by December 1967. Within the movement several veteran activists began to organize mobilization committees to mount large-scale demonstrations. Although these committees often fragmented over tactics and objectives, they did lead to action. On 15 April 1965, the so-called 'Spring Mobilization' in New York City's Central Park attracted 300,000 protesters, who then marched to the United Nations Building. The keynote speaker was Reverend Martin Luther King Jr., who had won a Nobel Peace Prize for his nonviolent campaign for the civil rights of African Americans. He denounced the war both for its violence and for its drain on public funds that could be better used to ease poverty and to improve public health and education.

The New York march also included a small group calling itself Vietnam Veterans Against the War. Also in April, 50,000 protesters rallied in San Francisco, where speakers urged young men to refuse to submit to the draft even if disobedience meant arrest and incarceration.

Over the summer a group calling itself the National Mobilization Committee, or the 'Mobe,' planned what became one of the most significant protest events of the war. On 21–22 October 1967, approximately 100,000 protesters assembled in Washington, DC, at the Lincoln Memorial, and then about half of them moved over to the Pentagon. The speeches during this mass demonstration ranged from standard liberal calls for negotiations to radical denunciations of the president of the United States as a war criminal. The activities of the crowd also varied from colorful antics, such as placing flowers in the barrels of rifles held by soldiers outside the Pentagon, to militant attempts to breach police lines. The latter resulted in some 700 arrests. Although it was not new to this particular demonstration, a frequent chant from the crowd was 'Hey, Hey, LBJ! How many kids did you kill today!'[3]

Although Johnson, and later President Richard Nixon, claimed that these rude and direct verbal assaults on the president and on US policy had no meaningful impact on decision making, the White House took great interest in the antiwar movement. Despite being a minority view, open dissent over the war raised the possibility of threatening the administration politically. Large street protests could also further destabilize public order that had already been rocked by civil rights protests and even acts of urban violence spawned by feelings of racial and economic injustice. Government officials became especially concerned that the peace movement aided the enemy. It seemed that mobs chanting in the streets could only encourage Hanoi to resist negotiations in the belief that the American people would ultimately pressure their own leaders into compromise. Johnson himself was convinced that communist or other foreign influences were behind the demonstrations because otherwise, 'Americans would not be behaving the way they are.' He pressed the FBI and CIA to investigate. In a detailed study, the CIA concluded that there was 'no significant evidence that would prove communist control or direction of the US peace movement or its leaders.'[4]

The existence of the movement affected the behavior of leaders, but it did not decide policy choices. Voices critical of ROLLING THUNDER, such as editorials in the *New York Times*, prompted Johnson to try to use bombing pauses as signals for negotiations. McNamara and other prominent administration figures limited their public appearances because of hecklers. The messages from the war's critics, however, were mixed and even contradictory. Dissenters called 'doves' divided into radicals who demanded that the United States unilaterally withdraw from Vietnam or liberals who argued for negotiations even if compromise might mean political success for Hanoi. There were also conservative critics, labeled 'hawks,' who advocated various military options to end the war, ranging from more troops and more bombing to invasion of North Vietnam. Yet another military option was to concentrate not on force against the PAVN, but greater security for the South Vietnamese through civic action and pacification. In other words, the critics of Johnson's conduct of the war offered no clear alternative course for American policy.

Following the large antiwar demonstrations in October 1967, Johnson decided to initiate a public relations campaign to convince the public that his approach of 'enough but not too much' was working in Vietnam. With the notable exception of McNamara, his closest advisers were telling the president that indeed this optimistic scenario was true. There was no outward sign of the high-level discussion prompted by McNamara's doubts. Prominent administration figures such as General Westmoreland and the president himself made confident public statements implying that victory was in sight. Public opinion polls showed some slipping of support for the war, but Johnson believed he could manage the issue politically as he had before. On 30 November, Senator Eugene McCarthy of Minnesota announced he would challenge Johnson for the Democratic nomination for president, but this relatively unknown senator, who had become outspoken against the war at the urging of CALCAV, seemed to pose no real challenge to Johnson. Without knowing that battlefield conditions in Vietnam would soon change, however, the president ordered a public relations effort that would compound his credibility problems with the American public in profound ways.

Tet

On 30 and 31 January 1968 as the Vietnamese were celebrating the biggest holiday of the year, the lunar new year celebration called Tet, Vietcong and People's Army of Vietnam (PAVN) forces launched coordinated assaults on important military and civilian targets throughout all of South Vietnam. The continuing vulnerability of the South to sudden collapse became alarmingly apparent in the heavy fighting that ensued. In one of the greatest military surprises since Pearl Harbor, NLF units simultaneously attacked dozens of urban areas and military installations. Guerrillas even breached the US embassy compound in Saigon for a few hours before being destroyed, but not before this suicide mission against the symbol of the American presence provided some sensational photos and news stories. After a few days of heavy fighting in many places, US troops and surprisingly resilient ARVN units countered the offensive. Only in Hue and the Saigon suburb of Cholon did intense fighting continue for about three weeks. Westmoreland claimed military success because the NLF failed in its goal to incite a popular uprising, many in the urban population actually rallied behind the government of Nguyen Van Thieu, no vital territory was permanently lost, and extremely heavy casualties were inflicted on the attackers.

The government in Hanoi believed that its strategy of protracted war was working because it had been able to survive the US escalation of bombing and numbers of troops since 1965, but leaders in the North perceived the American leadership as 'stubborn' and willing to inflict more damage on the DRV and its forces.[5] Consequently PAVN strategists had decided to speed up the process with a surprise, countrywide offensive. They believed that they could sufficiently destabilize the Republic of Vietnam (RVN) government and increase the cost of the war to Americans enough to lead Washington to give up on the idea of sustaining a government in Saigon. Their plan had worked well to a point. They created a major diversion with a siege of the US Marine base at Khe Sanh in northwestern South Vietnam. The build-up of PAVN strength around Khe Sanh and some other PAVN operations in remote areas had lured Military Assistance Command, Vietnam (MACV) into moving some US combat units away from the cities, the real targets of the offensive. These feints and the inability of US intelligence to discern the full significance of Vietcong movements toward the cities led to the surprise and initial successes of the Tet assaults. When the fighting ultimately ended, however, the communists' forces had suffered 45,000 casualties, and the Vietcong combat strength was so decimated that the PAVN had to take over most ground operations against the Americans and ARVN for the remainder of the war. These were serious losses, but Hanoi had made a psychological and political impact within the United States.

Based on news reports from Vietnam, many Americans concluded that Tet was a defeat or at least a reality check. Having heard the administration's assurances of progress in November, citizens interpreted the stunning magnitude of the offensive as evidence that the end was not near. Journalists and others expressed doubts that government claims about success could be trusted. Walter Cronkite of CBS News was one of the most respected members of the news media and had previously accepted official reports of progress. In a February special report from Vietnam, Cronkite declared that the war appeared to be a stalemate and that the time had come for negotiations. The Tet Offensive demonstrated that much more American blood and treasure would be lost even if Washington were able ultimately to convince Hanoi to accept a separate southern regime. Such additional costs, for many, were unacceptable. After Tet, more and more Americans simply wanted the United States out of Vietnam.[6]

A number of writers have advanced a 'stab in the back' argument, which alleges that the pessimistic reporting and analysis of the Tet fighting turned a military success into psychological defeat. Actually, Tet was a military as well as psychological defeat from which the US effort to impose its power on Vietnam never recovered. Despite Westmoreland's public confidence, military leaders privately acknowledged that the enemy offensive exposed serious weaknesses in the American war effort. The massive American air and ground war had not deterred infiltration into the South. The Tet combat weakened the ranks of the Vietcong, but the PAVN could and would continue to pour a virtually limitless supply of men into the RVN. US and ARVN losses had been high, and the fighting generated thousands of refugees, further destabilizing the South. In an 'eyes only' message to Westmoreland on 1 March, Army Chief of Staff General Harold K. Johnson concluded: 'We suffered a loss, there can be no doubt about it.'[7]

President Johnson was still not prepared to accept the idea of defeat in Vietnam, but he had from the beginning wanted to keep the war limited. The Tet Offensive raised the obvious question of whether the number of US military forces in Vietnam was enough to ever break the military stalemate, and this question became specific when General Earle Wheeler, chairman of the Joint Chiefs of Staff (JCS), supported a request to the president from Westmoreland for 206,000 more troops to mount a counteroffensive. Leaked almost immediately to the press, the troop request generated extremely negative responses from the antiwar movement and some members of Congress. Already sensitive to eroding public support and keenly aware of the approaching presidential election, Johnson turned to his new secretary of defense, Clark Clifford, for a thorough policy reevaluation.

Clifford had been a strong supporter of Johnson's Vietnam decisions, once US escalation had begun, and had just replaced the disillusioned McNamara. During February and early March he consulted with the JCS and with civilian officials in the Pentagon, most of whom were aware of

McNamara's misgivings about increasing the size of US forces. The new secretary began to realize as had his predecessor that there was no clear strategy for victory, that a military solution to the war remained elusive, and that simply adding more US troops was no guarantee of success. Outside government circles, press and popular opposition to the war was mounting, and many prominent businessmen were worrying openly about the damage that the war-generated government deficits and drain on American gold reserves were having on the national economy. Clifford arranged for Johnson to meet with the Wise Men on 26 March in a very different environment than the last meeting of that group of external advisers in November.

Prior to the meeting, the president told Clifford and other White House aides that he did not view the Tet Offensive as a defeat for the United States. What concerned him most was how the $5–7 billion of additional war costs associated with Westmoreland's request would take resources from his Great Society programs. On 24 March he authorized a deployment of only 13,500 additional troops. On the morning of the scheduled meeting with the Wise Men, he despaired to Wheeler and General Creighton Abrams, whom he has just named to succeed Westmoreland as chief of MACV, that 'our financial situation is abominable' and that Congress would cut spending on programs for 'poverty, housing and education' before it would raise taxes and increase war spending. He also shared with the generals his awareness of the political and public pressure:

> I don't give a damn about the election. I will be happy to keep doing what is right and lose the election. ... I will have overwhelming disapproval in the polls and elections. I will go down the drain. I don't want the whole alliance and military pulled in with it. ... *The Times* and *Post* are all against us. Most of the press is against us. ... We have no support for the war. This is caused by the 206,000 troop request, leaks, Ted Kennedy and Bobby Kennedy.[8]

As he had done since his initial escalation decisions in 1965, Johnson was trying to find a middle ground that would contain both the communists in Vietnam and his critics, both hawks and doves, at home.

On the afternoon of 26 March, Johnson and his key advisers met with the Wise Men, who had been briefed the evening before by General William DePuy, CIA analyst George Carver, and Ambassador Philip Habib. Although there were a few dissenting voices, the overwhelming majority of the Wise Men had significantly shifted their position from the November meeting. 'We can no longer do the job we set out to do in the time we have left and we must begin to take steps to disengage,' Dean Acheson summarized. From the briefing they had received, Arthur Dean added: 'We all got the impression that there is no military conclusion in sight. We felt time is running out.' Johnson responded with surprise to the directness of the recommendation for disengagement and wanted to hear the same briefing for himself. He ended the meeting with the reflection: 'Maybe I haven't gotten the whole story. I gather that it is different from what I have been getting top-side.'[9]

On 27 March, DePuy and Carver repeated their briefing for the president. He had difficulty understanding what they were saying and why it had led the Wise Men to their pessimistic conclusion. They were not contending that the war was lost or that there were not other possible military and diplomatic options to pursue. Similarly, Wheeler had not used a defeatist argument in support of Westmoreland's request for more soldiers. What both sides on the troop request debate were saying was that the current level of US effort promised only continued stalemate. The previous briefings that had assured the president that progress was being made had not served him well. The time had arrived to place a more precise value on the strategic worth of Vietnam to the United States. Further escalation would increase the cost to the United States, and negotiation would limit or reduce costs.[10]

Johnson weighed the two courses before the United States and went on national television on 31 March 1968 to discuss 'our search for peace in South Vietnam.' Noting the escalating cycle of violence, he declared that 'there is no need to delay the talks that could bring an end to this long and bloody war.' He announced that 'we are prepared to move immediately toward peace through negotiations,' and he named the veteran US diplomat W. Averell Harriman as his personal representative in these talks. As a sign of good faith, he revealed that he was ordering a restriction of the US bombing of North Vietnam to the area south of the twentieth parallel, that is, the region adjacent to the demilitarized zone (DMZ) dividing the DRV and RVN and well away from Hanoi. In the speech he also acknowledged the growing contention within the United States over the war. Noting that 'there is division in the American house now,' he asked all Americans 'to guard against divisiveness and all its ugly consequences.' Proclaiming that he would not allow 'the Presidency to become involved in partisan divisions,' he ended the address with the dramatic announcement that 'I shall not seek, and I will not accept, the nomination of my party for another term as your President.'[11]

Johnson was a master politician with much left to accomplish on his domestic agenda, but the war had forced him to relinquish the political power that he had always sought. The meetings in late March made him see that the DRV and NLF were too strong and his own base of support was too weak for him to continue to fight a war on the side while he tried to create his Great Society. He had attempted to pursue a policy of what the journalists dubbed 'guns and butter.' He aimed to achieve success in implementing social and economic reform at home and in containing communism in Vietnam before he stood for reelection, and time had run out. He convinced himself that by withdrawing from the race early his historical reputation could be salvaged. As he told biographer Doris Kearns after he left office, he thought that history would record that 'he acted nobly at this critical moment.'[12] The war itself, however, was far from over.

Combat without compromise

Despite the conciliatory tone of Johnson's 31 March speech, his administration was far from ready to compromise with Hanoi. Although the DRV surprised Washington by agreeing quickly to begin talks in Paris, both sides continued to wage heavy combat believing that their adversary was weakened. In March and April, 42 US and 37 ARVN battalions conducted two massive ground operations to clear remaining Vietcong forces from the area around Saigon. On 5 May the Vietcong launched new attacks on Saigon in a so-called 'mini-Tet Offensive' intended, like the original offensive, to destabilize the RVN regime. Again there was fierce fighting that ended with heavy losses to the Vietcong. During the summer, elements of the US Army's 7th Cavalry and the 101st Airborne Division were airlifted via helicopters into the A Shau Valley west of Hue. The valley was a strongly defended PAVN base area near the border with Laos. The helicopters received heavy antiaircraft fire, but few North Vietnamese regulars were found as the main forces slipped into Laos. US Marines inflicted heavy casualties on PAVN units in the area of the DMZ, especially near Con Thien in October. When 1968 came to an end, it had been the bloodiest year of the war for American troops with more than 14,000 killed and 150,000 wounded. Even with the air campaign against North Vietnam reduced, US bombing in South Vietnam and adjacent areas exceeded one million tons during the year. Yet despite all this violence, the war remained a stalemate.[13]

The frustrating and violent nature of the ground war increasingly placed American troops fighting it in moral as well as physical jeopardy. Infantry searches for guerrilla fighters regularly took heavily armed young Americans into villages and rice fields where they came into direct contact with civilian noncombatants. On these patrols, US soldiers fell victim to sniper fire, land mines, and booby traps. The unseen enemy behind these lethal weapons may or may not have been the villagers themselves, who in turn may or may not have been willing supporters of the Vietcong. A combination of fear and rage and possible commendation for 'body count' led some officers and their men into indiscriminate acts of violence against unarmed civilians, including women, small children, and old men.

The worst known single case of this phenomenon was the My Lai massacre that occurred in the aftermath of Tet. On 16 March 1968, two American companies killed 504 unresisting men, women, and children in the hamlets of My Lai and My Khe in Quang Ngai province. The incident was covered up for over a year until Ron Ridenhour, a soldier who was not involved but knew of the event, was able to prompt an investigation. Although several soldiers and their superior officers were implicated in this atrocity, the military justice system was able to convict only one lieutenant for murder. Prosecution was difficult because of the cover-up and the ambiguity of whether these men were individually accountable or should be treated as simply cogs in a war machine. In another case, an elite reconnaissance unit repeatedly brutalized and killed civilians in the same province over a seven-month period in 1967, and despite four and a half years of investigation there were no successful prosecutions. Two and a half million American soldiers were in Vietnam during the war, and the overwhelming majority served honorably. Criminal acts occur in all wars, and sentences for murder, rape, and assault were obtained in Vietnam. The incidents of atrocity and their cover-ups, however, raised fundamental questions about the mission and discipline of ground operations in what had begun as a war for the political security of the Saigon government. Westmoreland's attrition strategy seemed ill suited to that goal.[14]

In June 1968, General Creighton Abrams officially replaced Westmoreland as MACV commander and began to shift US strategy from attrition to greater use of small-unit operations, an accelerated pacification program, and Vietnamization, that is, improving the ARVN's ability to do more of the fighting. As deputy commander of MACV in 1967, he had worked to make the ARVN a more effective force, and the performance of Saigon's troops during the Tet Offensive was a credit to his leadership. As head of MACV, he increased the size of the South's army to 800,000 and provided it more modern equipment and increased training. Quantity could not translate quickly into quality, however, and many old problems remained. Morale was poor in many units, and qualified officers were hard to find. By 1968, the combat operations had become so Americanized that the natural tendency of many South Vietnamese military leaders was simply to hold back and let the Americans do it. This situation produced tension between the allies as American forces often perceived the ARVN as slackers and the South Vietnamese viewed the Americans as patronizing.

Like Vietnamization, pacification was also a slow and arduous effort. Neither MACV nor the Saigon government had placed much effort on securing rural areas before 1968. With the Vietcong fighting strength weakened by Tet, RVN officials were able to make inroads into some areas. The Civilian Operations and Revolutionary Development Support (CORDS) initiative started in 1967 had never been well organized. Under its auspices, the Chieu Hoi program enticed some Vietcong defectors to the government side with promises of amnesty, and the Phoenix program arrested some other enemy cadre. The clandestine Communist Party structure remained in place in the South, however. In Saigon itself, the Thieu government showed some signs of dealing with long-standing problems of inflation and corruption, but the huge problem of refugees created by the Tet fighting went largely unaddressed. The Saigon regime, as in the past, sparked little enthusiasm among the population.[15]

While the military and political stalemate persisted in South Vietnam, a diplomatic process of sorts began in Paris on 13 May 1968 when Harriman met formally for the first time with Xuan Thuy of the DRV. The two sides remained far apart. They wrangled for weeks over procedural questions about the participation of the RVN and NLF in the talks – Harriman's formula of referring to 'ourside' and 'yourside' became the solution – and even over the shape of the conference table. Although Harriman, with Clifford's support, wanted to suggest a bombing pause and a mutual ceiling on troops to get real negotiations going, the White House decided on starting from a tough stance. Rusk, Rostow, Westmoreland, and Ambassador Elsworth Bunker in Saigon believed that the Tet fighting had weakened Hanoi's position and that firmness was in order.

Already skeptical of North Vietnam's willingness to compromise, Johnson sided with the hard liners. His instincts about Hanoi were basically correct. The Politburo had adopted a 'fighting while negotiating' strategy. Its intention was not to offer any concessions but to use the talks to strengthen its position, if possible, by prolonging the announced limits on the air war, encouraging the antiwar movement in America, and fomenting distrust between Washington and Saigon over possible terms. The DRV stuck with its past position that no substantive talks were possible as long as any US bombing or other acts of war continued in Vietnam. At the first National Security Council meeting after the start of the formal talks, Johnson summarized: 'There is no evidence that the North Vietnamese will negotiate seriously. They will do no more than remain in Paris to talk rather than negotiate until the next Administration takes over.'[16]

Election of 1968

While the dying continued in Vietnam and the diplomacy sputtered in Paris, the American political process went through its quadrennial selection of a president. The war was, of course, a significant issue with over 500,000 Americans in South Vietnam, an average of 400 per week being killed through the first half of 1968, and news reports and visual images of the conflict appearing nightly on television. The questions raised by the Tet fighting seemed to have opened the war to debate. Would the political campaign become a referendum on the war?

Vietnam was not the only policy question on voters' minds, however, and the election outcome was not necessarily going to determine the course of the war. Citizens were divided over whether Johnson's ambitious War on Poverty was costing taxpayers too much or was in fact going underfunded and adding unfulfilled expectations to the existing burdens of the dispossessed. Pent-up frustrations of the poor and powerless living in economically depressed inner-city neighborhoods of some of America's largest cities had led to major outbursts of violence in the summers of 1965, 1966, and 1967. Motivated by positive expressions of black pride and negative expressions of anger at local economic and political conditions, many African Americans in cities such as Los Angeles, Detroit, and Newark had struck out with arson, looting, and violence against the urban ghettos. Pitched battles with police and national guardsmen, usually predominately white, had resulted in scores of deaths, hundreds of arrests, and millions of dollars in property damage. Combined with the less violent but unsettling actions of antiwar protesters, the urban riots made 'law and order' a prime campaign issue in 1968. For many voters 'law and order' meant a desire for authorities to take steps against African American militants and peace demonstrators.

It was the war, however, and specifically the public reaction to the Tet Offensive that made it possible for members of Johnson's own Democratic Party to step forward and challenge the powerful incumbent for the presidential nomination. The initial beneficiary of this change in political climate was Senator Eugene McCarthy. When he had announced in November 1967 his antiwar candidacy for the Democratic nomination, he was acting on behalf of so-called 'reform' Democrats or concerned Democrats, who disagreed with the president's continued escalation of the American war and who favored negotiations. They sought to use the conventional political process to make their point, but had little real hope of actually dislodging Johnson from the White House. These party insurgents would have preferred to back Senator Robert Kennedy of New York, the slain president's brother, who was known to favor negotiations and who was much stronger than McCarthy as a serious candidate. Kennedy had no fondness for Johnson or his war policies, but the senator did not want to appear disloyal to the president in wartime nor to be causing further division at home when American soldiers were dying abroad. More importantly, Kennedy expected to be the party's nominee for president in 1972, and a premature and unsuccessful political move against the incumbent in 1968 could dash those plans.

In February following the Tet Offensive, public opinion polls began to show for the first time that about half of the public believed US military intervention in Vietnam had been a mistake. Inspired by this data, liberal activists within the Democratic Party began to work actively in support of McCarthy in New Hampshire, the site of the first primary election of the year. The senator was himself a lackadaisical and aloof campaigner, but thousands of college students converged upon New Hampshire to canvass the state on his behalf. Admonished by savvy political advisors to 'Be Clean for Gene,' the young men were clean shaven and wore coats and ties, and the young women dressed conservatively without miniskirts or exotic jewelry. Hollywood celebrities, such as actors Tony Randall and Paul Newman, drew crowds to McCarthy rallies. In his campaign speeches, McCarthy took a moderate stand on the war, urging negotiations, but he also took a pointed position on social issues, criticizing the president for failing to deliver results on fundamental problems of race, class, urbanization, and economic equality.

When the voting took place on 12 March, Johnson suffered a stunning defeat. Political analysts had predicted that McCarthy would get less than 20 percent of the vote, but on election day he got 42 percent.

Since Johnson had not bothered even to file as a candidate, a hasty effort before the election by the state Democratic organization produced a write-in vote of 49 percent for the president. A final tally of all write-in votes after the election determined that McCarthy had actually out polled the president by about 200 votes. Additional follow-up analysis of the vote revealed another surprise in addition to this dramatic victory by a previously little-known senator over a president who had won a landslide victory in 1964. Polling data indicated that more people had voted for McCarthy who were hawks that favored a stronger US military effort in Vietnam than were doves who favored military withdrawal. In other words, the outcome in New Hampshire was a strong anti-Johnson vote that had exposed his political vulnerability to criticism from both hawks and doves.[17]

A season of political shocks had now begun as Robert Kennedy announced his candidacy for the Democratic nomination four days after the New Hampshire vote. McCarthy and many of his supporters, both his ardent young campaigners and those who had organized them, resented this seemingly arrogant and exploitative move, which suggested that Kennedy had allowed others to take the risk of challenging the incumbent and that he would now try to reap the reward of their courage. There was considerable accuracy in this complaint, but there was also more to the story. Since the outbreaks of the urban rioting in 1965, Kennedy had been receiving an education on domestic tension in the country and had been growing in his own social consciousness. He generally agreed with much of the indictment that McCarthy and others were making that Johnson's Great Society had not relieved the nation's domestic ills, in large part because of the war. He also agreed with the widely held opinion in the wake of the Tet Offensive that the high level of destructiveness of American power and the low level of credibility of the Saigon government made continued US intervention difficult to justify. Not having forthrightly confronted Johnson on these points before McCarthy's victory, however, understandably made his belated candidacy appear opportunistic.

In the wake of McCarthy's upset victory and Kennedy's announcement, Johnson made his speech of 31 March disclosing that he would not be a candidate for reelection. The president could almost assuredly have used his powers of incumbency and his enormous skills as a political power broker to secure the party's nomination. McCarthy and Kennedy had not intimidated him into withdrawing. He had arrived at his decision independently, but he retained a keen interest in who his successor would be and what policies that person would pursue. He had as low a regard for McCarthy and Kennedy as they had for him. Johnson had generally isolated his vice president, Hubert H. Humphrey, from Vietnam policy making, but shortly before delivery of the 31 March speech, the president showed the text to Humphrey. After the vice president finished reading, Johnson said, 'You'd better start planning your campaign for President.' Subdued, Humphrey replied, 'There's no way I can beat the Kennedys.'[18]

The next shock was quick in coming when, on 4 April, Martin Luther King Jr. fell victim to a white assassin's bullet in Memphis, Tennessee. Just at a moment when the Tet fighting and Johnson's dramatic speech had seemed to start to focus political discourse on the war abroad, the reality of violence and division at home came rushing back to center stage. With racial tensions already inflamed from the previous spasms of urban warfare, news of the assassination touched off another round of destruction, deaths, and arrests in over 100 cities. While preparing to speak at a previously scheduled campaign appearance in an African American neighborhood in Indianapolis on the evening of 4 April, Kennedy received the report of the murder. He chose to break the news himself to the crowd and proceeded to make an impassioned, and for that night successful, appeal for an end to violence, which had also victimized his family. In his remarks that evening he reflected: 'In this difficult time for the United States, it is perhaps well to ask what kind of a nation we are and what direction we want to move in.'[19] In that sentence he captured the foreign and domestic context in which the presidential election of that year was placed.

Through April and May the contest for the Democratic nomination continued, and Kennedy chose to make his questions about America's national identity his campaign theme. Turmoil was everywhere with urban violence in the wake of King's death, heavy fighting continuing in Vietnam, and antiwar radicalism seemingly on the rise. Student protesters forcibly occupied the administrative offices of Columbia University in New York City; radicals burned the Reserve Officer Training Corps (ROTC) building at Stanford University in California; and a group of veteran agitators who created the Youth International Party or Yippies (a variation of the countercultural term Hippies) had announced satirically that they would nominate a pig named Pigasus for president. Having started earlier with an announced candidacy, McCarthy won some additional state primaries, but Kennedy was rapidly gaining momentum with a vigorously waged, often emotional campaign that championed social and economic justice. Many reform Democrats and college students followed Kennedy's lead, but others remained loyal to McCarthy, who like them was wary of the Kennedy clan's reputation for ruthless ambition. On the subject of the war, both men were moderate critics advocating negotiations and not unilateral US withdrawal from Vietnam.

On 4 June Kennedy's pursuit of the nomination seemed to be gaining its stride when he won the California primary and with it 174 delegate votes at the Democratic convention. He defeated McCarthy by four percentage points, and Humphrey trailed as a distant third. Kennedy had captured the African American and Hispanic vote but had also gained valuable help from the state's Democratic leaders. His courting of political bosses and his moderation on the war issue had troubled many youthful and reform Democrats who continued to favor McCarthy. Still, Kennedy seemed on his way to the nomination when the unbelievable happened. Leaving a celebration at a Los Angeles hotel the night of his victory, he was shot and killed by a lone assassin with a handgun. The assailant was immediately arrested, but the motive, if any, for the killing was and remains unclear.

Kennedy's death stunned the nation. For the second time in two months an assassin's bullet had killed a national leader, and for the second time in less than five years brutal murder had visited the highly visible and admired Kennedy family. Preservation of law and order, already present because of the violent clashes in the cities and the disorderly conduct of war protesters, and de-escalation of the war were now two key questions on which voters looked to the presidential candidates for answers. With Kennedy gone, the leading candidate on the Democratic side now became Vice President Humphrey.

Although McCarthy had fared much better as a candidate than he or any of his antiwar supporters had ever expected, he could not match the depth of support that Humphrey had where it would count at the national nominating convention, that is, with the key figures in the regular Democratic Party organization. Under party rules, the delegates chosen through the state primaries were significantly outnumbered by delegates chosen through local and state party committees, whose power and position depended upon the president and vice president as national party heads. Through these connections, Humphrey could and eventually did secure the nomination for president. As a major party candidate for the highest political office in the land, however, the vice president faced serious dilemmas on both the war issue and the law and order issue.

As a member of the US Senate from Minnesota, Humphrey had been well known as a typical, even archetypical, liberal Democrat. In the tradition of Harry Truman, John Kennedy, and Lyndon Johnson, he was identified with the progressive legacy of the New Deal. He had been especially courageous among national leaders in his championing of civil rights protection for African Americans. He became Johnson's running mate in 1964 because of his loyal and heartfelt support for the president's Great Society program. As was characteristic of liberal Democrats, he was a staunch anticommunist and defender of the containment policy. As vice president he was closely connected in the public's mind with the administration's domestic policies and its conduct of the war.

Therein lay his dilemma. Like Senator William Fulbright and some other liberal Democrats, Humphrey had come to doubt the validity of making Vietnam a test of containment and had grown concerned about how the war was diverting US resources from domestic and other international needs. After Humphrey privately questioned the administration's course in Vietnam, Johnson had excluded him from White House policy discussions. In an effort not to alienate the many party regulars who continued to support Johnson on the war, Humphrey entered the campaign for the nomination saddled with apparent agreement with the president despite his personal conviction that more should be done to seek negotiations. Also, as polls indicated a growing concern among voters about law and order, Humphrey had to restrain his instincts to defend liberal causes such as civil rights activism and the rights of peace advocates to mount public protests. He could not afford to appear soft on law and order. If he openly opposed current war policy, he would be tagged as disloyal to his own administration and would further separate himself from Johnson and the many party leaders allied with Johnson. Thus he worked through the party organization for the nomination while avoiding clear public positions on key issues.

As the Democratic National Convention began in Chicago in August, Humphrey had enough delegate support to be nominated, but delegates who had backed Kennedy, McCarthy, and another peace candidate, Senator George McGovern of South Dakota, tried to insert a plank in the platform calling for an end to US bombing and for a coalition government in South Vietnam. The Humphrey delegates blocked this direct challenge to the president's policies, although the vice president's personal views were close to the proposed language. Humphrey then won the nomination on the first ballot, but events outside the convention hall overshadowed the formal business. Thousands of mostly young antiwar protesters had descended upon Chicago and were in the streets and parks expressing their views in various ways throughout the convention. Most of the demonstrators were peaceful, but some radicals associated with the Yippies or SDS antagonized the police. Democratic

Mayor Richard J. Daley had vowed that disruption and protest would not be tolerated in his city and had assembled thousands of police and national guardsmen. On the night of 28 August as the roll call of states confirmed Humphrey as the party's nominee, a massive riot began. Protesters attempted to march near the convention hall, and some of the police responded with excessive use of clubs, mace, and other violence. Hundreds of injuries and arrests occurred. As television cameras recorded and broadcast this extreme outburst of contention over the war, some of the marchers were chanting, 'The whole world is watching.'[20]

One of the most interested members of the television audience watching this spectacle was Richard M. Nixon, the Republican nominee for president. With the Democrats deeply divided and Humphrey associated with Johnson's unpopular policies, Republican prospects for victory in November seemed good. Complicating the major party confrontation was the presence of a third-party contender, Governor George Wallace of Alabama. A self-styled populist and segregationist, Wallace criticized Johnson's civil rights policies and was outspoken in his disdain for unruly protesters of all types. His potential to take white voters away from both major parties made his candidacy significant, but he had no real national campaign organization with which to actually win the election. He also had a controversial vice presidential running mate, General Curtis LeMay, whose casual talk about use of atomic weapons frightened many people.

Nixon was a strong but somewhat surprising presidential contender. After serving for eight years as Dwight Eisenhower's vice president, he lost election to the presidency only by the narrowest of margins to John Kennedy in 1960. After an unsuccessful run for governor of California in 1962, he had bitterly denounced the press for its treatment of him and announced his political retirement. A man with what many characterized as ruthless political ambition, Nixon could not, however, resist the attraction of the political arena and especially pursuit of the presidency. Through the mid-1960s, he supported local and state Republican candidates in their campaigns throughout the country and built up a solid party base. By 1968 he had emerged from what had seemed political oblivion and easily gained his party's nomination for president.

Nixon not only overcame the perception that he was a political loser, but he managed to create a 'new Nixon' image. When he began his political career after the Second World War, he rode to national notice as a right-wing Republican and a Red-baiter ready to defend America against communists at home and abroad. By the mid-1960s he had softened his tone a bit, but it was clear that he loathed protesters and considered demonstrators a threat to public safety and national security. Repeatedly and with good effect, he assured voters that he was the law and order candidate. On the issue of Vietnam, he also interpreted the public mood very well. He had consistently supported the decisions of Eisenhower, Kennedy, and Johnson to defend South Vietnam, but he also understood that in 1968 the public was growing weary of that commitment.

In his campaign speeches, he made vague, sweeping statements that, as president, he would bring 'peace with honor' to Vietnam, and he allowed the press to report that he had a 'secret plan' to end the war. He actually had no plan, and he was in many respects an unlikely peace candidate. As a congressional critic of Truman's alleged loss of China in 1949, Nixon had been militant in his commitment to America's pledge to oppose communist tyranny. As vice president in 1954, he had urged a hesitant Eisenhower to use US troops or air power in Indochina to aid the French. After losing the presidential contest to Kennedy in 1960, Nixon publicly supported Kennedy's subsequent decision to increase US aid to Vietnam. When controversy swirled around Johnson in 1967, Nixon wrote that 'without the American commitment in Vietnam, Asia would be a far different place today.'[21] He not only had voiced approval of Johnson's military escalation in Vietnam but had, in fact, often complained that Johnson should have used greater US force, especially air power. He had chastised the incumbent for paying too much attention to dissenters and thus being overly cautious. Nixon continued to reaffirm the domino theory that Eisenhower had stated when Nixon was vice president. The Republican candidate insisted that the aggression of North Vietnam against South Vietnam was part of a global Soviet and Chinese menace to international security and that the credibility of the United States to deter that threat in Southeast Asia and in the world was as important as ever. What he meant by 'peace with honor' may have been ambiguous, but it did not mean devaluing the strategic importance of South Vietnam.

While the United States went through the tumultuous 1968 election to choose Johnson's successor, the administration's negotiations in Paris went nowhere. In late September, Humphrey was trailing Nixon by 20 points in the polls, and the candidate knew that he had to somehow escape from Johnson's shadow. In a speech in Salt Lake City, he inserted a sentence that if elected, 'I would stop the bombing as an acceptable risk for peace.'[22] Humphrey's standing in the polls and the financial contributions to his campaign rose significantly. His public signal about possible interest in a bombing halt also enabled Ambassador Harriman in Paris to get some movement from the North Vietnamese on the stalled negotiations. Hanoi's diplomats indicated for the first time that they would talk directly with representatives of Thieu's Saigon government if the bombing stopped. Although he personally doubted Hanoi's sincerity, Johnson made a televised statement on 31 October that all bombing of North Vietnam would stop and talks would begin on 6 November, the day after the election.

Thieu immediately made a public announcement that he would not participate in any direct talks with the DRV, and the White House had to follow with a statement that the start of talks would be delayed. Even without South Vietnamese obstruction, meaningful diplomatic progress was unlikely at that point. Johnson had consistently refused to retreat from the long-standing US opposition to recognition of the NLF and creation of a coalition government in the South. The DRV and NLF had successfully withstood the large-scale Americanization of the war and gave no indication of being prepared to compromise.[23]

On election day, 5 November, Nixon eked out a narrow victory with 43.4 percent of the popular vote. Humphrey had 42.7 percent. The timing of Johnson's bombing-halt announcement on the eve of the election had raised the possibility of a last-minute, come-from-behind victory by Humphrey, and Thieu's public opposition may well have ended that hope. Behind the scenes was some unseemly intrigue. Johnson had not helped Humphrey during the campaign (which had a mixed impact on the candidate's prospects), and the president was, in fact, furious about Humphrey's position on bombing after his Salt Lake City speech. Some people close to Johnson thought he actually wanted Nixon to win. Johnson claimed that his 31 October announcement was diplomacy not politics, but he was well aware that it helped Humphrey. Johnson knew from illegal wiretaps that the Nixon campaign was in communication with Thieu to prevent any diplomatic breakthroughs before the election that would help the Democrats. This information outraged Johnson. The Democrats could have publicly revealed that the Republicans were trying to sabotage the peace talks for political advantage but chose not to do so.[24]

The last minute maneuvering and the war itself were significant but not the only reasons why Nixon won. Voters had complaints about the Johnson–Humphrey administration because of the Indochina conflict, but many citizens were also uneasy about the forced pace of the Great Society reforms, inflation, and violence in the streets. Nixon had campaigned for the presidency pledging to bring 'peace with honor' in Vietnam. He felt honor-bound by the concepts of commitment and credibility that had influenced Kennedy and Johnson before him. If he was going to find a way to 'de-Americanize' the war as he had often pledged during the campaign, he was going to have to be concerned, too, about the risks and consequences if the United States left South Vietnam to stand unsteadily on its own.

5

Consequences: Richard Nixon's War

During the 1968 presidential campaign, Richard Nixon had pledged to bring the war to a 'successful conclusion.'[1] However 'success' might be defined by the end of 1968, for most Americans it meant in one way or another to get US ground forces out of Vietnam. Despite that understanding, President Nixon continued the US military involvement for four more years as he searched for an honorable exit that would preserve his own and the nation's credibility. Upon taking office, Nixon and his chief national security aide Henry Kissinger knew that the voters expected them to end US military intervention in Vietnam. They interpreted that mandate, however, as requiring them to find a way to maintain US credibility. In their estimation, simply to pull out would have far-ranging domestic and international consequences. Nixon himself had been part of the conservative Republican chorus that had heaped partisan condemnation on Harry Truman for supposedly 'losing China' without a fight in 1949. To abandon the Republic of Vietnam (RVN) to an overt takeover by the communist Democratic Republic of Vietnam (DRV) would have a 'terrible' political impact and 'destroy' his administration in his view.[2] Similarly, Nixon and Kissinger believed that America's friends and enemies abroad would be closely watching how the United States extricated itself from the war. Kissinger maintained resolutely that the 'peace of the world' and the stability of 'international order' depended on the ability of the United States to end the war with its honor and credibility as a world power intact.[3]

Like the administrations that preceded them, Nixon and Kissinger began with a certainty that American power was the key to success and that US military might could still coerce the DRV into a compromise settlement for the mutual withdrawal of US and North Vietnamese forces from South Vietnam and leave the existing government of the RVN in place. Ultimately, however, it was Washington, not Hanoi, that made the key concession – the acknowledgment that the Vietnamese would determine their own fate. Kennedy had attempted counter-insurgency warfare, and Johnson had waged combat to sustain the Saigon regime, but it was Nixon who finally accepted compromise. It was a compromise that allowed the government headed by Nguyen Van Thieu to remain in Saigon, but that also allowed the forces of North Vietnam to remain in the South. This arrangement effectively created a separation or an interval between the termination of US military inter-vention in Vietnam and whatever final political settlement the North and South would reach.

More bombs and fewer troops

In 1969, the US war effort remained massive, but the basic decision to de-escalate had already been reached. All of the major candidates for president in 1968 had tried to respond to that message from public opin-ion, and Nixon, as the victor, now had to try to deliver on his campaign assurances. He had no specific steps in mind, despite the impression generated during the campaign of a secret Nixon plan to end the war, but he was determined not to let the war drag him down as it had done to Johnson. To protect himself from that kind of political damage, he told his White House chief of staff H. R. 'Bob' Haldeman: 'I'm going to stop the war. Fast.'[4]

As a critic of Johnson's gradual escalation of pressure on North Vietnam, Nixon had often urged that the United States make greater use of its air power. When Hubert Humphrey had begun to attract support during the campaign with talk of a bombing halt, candidate Nixon had charged that bombing was 'the only trump card' US negotiators had.[5] On 31 October Johnson had indeed ceased Operation ROLLING THUNDER, the regular air attacks against targets in North Vietnam that had begun in 1965. This air campaign had destroyed more than half of the bridges in the DRV, most of the North's petroleum storage, and two-thirds of its electrical power plants and had killed an estimated 50,000 people, but it had not produced diplomatic concessions from Hanoi.[6] Although US air operations continued in Indochina in support of American ground forces in South Vietnam, could the new president, after having pledged to de-Americanize the war, resume a controversial and questionably effective bombardment of the DRV? Would such a campaign produce any faster results than it had for Johnson?

To help him devise a 'fast' solution to what seemed America's intractable problem of imposing a political settlement on Vietnam that would preserve a government in Saigon friendly to US strategic interests, Nixon turned to Dr Henry Kissinger, Harvard professor of international relations, who would serve as special assistant to the president for national security affairs. Unlike Haldeman and other top White House aides who had been key lieutenants in Nixon's political battles to gain the presidency, Kissinger had won his way into candidate Nixon's confidence in part by secretly supplying him confidential information about the Paris peace talks gained through personal contacts. Nixon and Kissinger were from different backgrounds – the professional politician from small-town America and the German-born, Ivy League intellectual – but they shared a common *realpolitik* approach to world affairs and a global vision of American power. Both were ambitious loners, but they recognized a need for each other. Nixon considered himself a foreign policy expert but wanted someone to help him implement his grand designs, and Kissinger needed the personal and intellectual access to power that Nixon could provide. Perhaps most significant, both men thrived on secrecy and intrigue. If Nixon were going to devise quickly a successful American exit from Vietnam, the two were prepared to act on their own, involving as few people from the administration, Congress, or the interested public as possible.

Over the first six months of the new administration, Nixon and Kissinger began to articulate a policy, but despite their self-images as grand strategists, there was a large element of improvisation in it. With the ground war stalemated and the option of deploying more US infantry forces politically unacceptable, the White House planners turned to secret diplomacy and to secret air bombardment of neutral Cambodia. They communicated to Hanoi a series of proposals that Kissinger later characterized as the same as the 'dove' plank that had been rejected at the Democratic Convention. Basically it was a two-tiered approach in which the United States and the DRV would negotiate a mutual withdrawal of forces from the RVN while the Saigon government and the National Liberation Front (NLF) discussed 'political reconciliation.' Kissinger thought this position would demonstrate flexibility to both Hanoi and the Democrats. In retrospect, he wrote: 'We were naively wrong in both expectations. Hanoi wanted victory, not compromise. At the same time several of the newly retired officials of the previous administration did not feel inhibited ... from adding to public pressures with proposals of their own.'[7]

To attempt to coerce Hanoi into movement toward a settlement, Nixon had Kissinger inform the government of the Soviet Union, the

DRV's principal industrial supplier, that any improvement in US–USSR relations would only come after the end of the war in Vietnam. Perhaps Moscow would place a premium on superpower harmony and put pressure on Hanoi. Nixon and Kissinger referred to this tactic as 'linkage.' Nixon also ordered the US Air Force to conduct attacks, including use of B-52 bombers, on so-called 'People's Army of Vietnam (PAVN) sanctuaries' in neutral Cambodia along the border with South Vietnam. Some of these attacks were followed by quick Special Forces ground strikes across the border. The White House ordered that these air and ground operations into Cambodia be kept strictly secret to avoid political backlash at home. When a story about the secret bombing of Cambodia appeared in the *New York Times*, Nixon and Kissinger had wiretaps placed on the telephones of National Security Council staff members to stop leaks to the press. This pattern of secrecy, illegal operations, and domestic spying in the early weeks of the administration set in motion a widening web of covert political actions that would ultimately lead to the Watergate scandals that would end Nixon's presidency.

The initial diplomatic and military moves did not produce the desired quick response from Hanoi, but they were part of a strategy known as the 'madman theory.' The concept was not new and had precedents in John Foster Dulles's 'brinkmanship' of the 1950s with implied threats of using nuclear weapons and in Theodore Roosevelt's 'big stick' demonstrations of US naval power at the beginning of the twentieth century. The term 'madman' came from a conversation Haldeman reported having with Nixon in late 1968: 'I call it the Madman Theory, Bob. I want the North Vietnamese to believe I've reached the point where I might do *anything* to stop the war. We'll slip the word to them that, "for God's sake, you know Nixon is obsessed about Communism. We can't restrain him when he's angry – and he has his hand on the nuclear button" – and Ho Chi Minh himself will be in Paris in two days begging for peace.'[8] Nixon's idea, to which Kissinger agreed, was to insert a significant element of unpredictability, intimidation, and even fury into US negotiating positions that would crack the opponent's resolve. It was meant to signal a departure from Johnson's rational approach of slow but steady increases in military pressure (enough but not too much) to the creation of an irrational context in which there were no apparent limits to the amount of pressure. Nixon's well-known reputation for political ruthlessness and risk taking enhanced the potential psychological impact on Hanoi, but signs of this behavior also troubled American observers who worried about what the president might do if the North Vietnamese remained as unresponsive as they were in the early months of 1969.[9]

Like the diplomatic efforts, the ground war in the South was also stymied. In May 1969 the 101st Airborne Division fought and won a major ten-day battle at Hamburger Hill in the A Shau Valley. The Americans suffered over 50 killed, but dislodged two North Vietnamese Army (NVA) battalions only to have the hard-won ridge abandoned a few days later. Such experiences devastated morale among US troops and created open dissension in the ranks. Hamburger Hill marked the end of the erstwhile attrition strategy. The related pacification program was no better. US troops would move into an area, and NLF political activity would vanish only to reappear immediately upon the relocation of the American unit. As one American official candidly observed: 'It is only occupation, not pacification.'[10]

With a military or diplomatic victory in any traditional sense continuing to elude Washington and the American death toll in the war still mounting, Nixon began to herald the policy of Vietnamization as the way to a successful conclusion of the American war in Vietnam. A larger and better equipped South Vietnamese military force was in the process of creation. On 8 June the White House announced the withdrawal of 25,000 US troops from South Vietnam, made possible supposedly because of the improved capability of the ARVN. In fact, South Vietnam's armed forces remained as problem-plagued as ever with poor leadership, corruption, and low morale prevalent throughout. Shortly before his troop reduction announcement, Nixon had met with President Nguyen Van Thieu at Midway Island, had praised the RVN leadership, and renewed the pledge of continued US support. Speaking with journalists in Guam soon afterward, the president made more sweeping statements, which eventually came to be called the Nixon Doctrine, that US policy would be to provide military and economic assistance to Asian nations fighting insurrections, but that those governments would provide their own soldiers.

Although the administration presented Vietnamization as a sign of progress in South Vietnam, it was more accurately a response to domestic opinion in the United States. Reducing the participation of US troops in the ground war would lower US casualties and decrease some, perhaps much, of the public outcry against the war. The White House hoped that it would be a sign to doves that the president was delivering on his campaign pledge to de-Americanize the war, but that it would also reassure hawks that the US commitment to the support of South Vietnam remained strong.

To try to keep DRV military pressure off the South as US troop levels declined, the administration continued with the madman concept. In

July, it leaked to the press dire threats of a 'go for broke' air and naval assault on the North – possibly including nuclear weapons. Through diplomatic channels, Nixon sent a personal message to the aging Ho Chi Minh that resembled an ultimatum. It set 1 November as a deadline for evidence of progress in negotiations or the United States would use 'measures of great consequence and great force.' The National Security Council staff also went to work under Kissinger's leadership on a plan for 'savage and punishing blows' against the DRV. Code-named DUCK HOOK, this contingency plan included saturation bombing of North Vietnam, a naval blockade of the North, and the mining of the principal DRV port of Haiphong.[11]

Kissinger began secret meetings on 4 August with North Vietnamese representatives in Paris hoping to arrange a diplomatic breakthrough. Hanoi's leaders refused to be intimidated by Nixon's rhetoric and continued to demand US withdrawal from the South and abandonment of its support of Thieu. On 15 August, and only two weeks before his death, Ho Chi Minh replied to Nixon's letter. The legendary revolutionary ignored the ultimatum and rejected compromise. The Politburo was calling Nixon's bluff. The DRV's stubbornness enraged the president, but his advisors, especially Secretary of Defense Melvin Laird, convinced him that a 'savage' attack on the North would not produce diplomatic results and would inflame antiwar protest in the United States, which had been relatively quiet in the beginning months of the administration.

Like Johnson, Nixon claimed that the peace movement did not influence his policy choices, but as an experienced politician always thinking of the consequences of his actions for the next election, he could not ignore such a significant expression of opinion. Demonstrations in the summer of 1969 had drawn smaller numbers than previous years, but the activists were far from finished. On 15 October, veterans of the McCarthy and Kennedy campaigns and other liberals staged the largest national protest to date – the Moratorium. In hundreds of cities that day, hundreds of thousands of Americans participated in mostly peaceful and dignified expressions of opposition to the war. The three national television networks – ABC, CBS, and NBC – devoted almost their entire evening news programs to coverage of the collage of activities ranging from the 250,000 who assembled in New York City's Central Park to a gathering of students at California's Whittier College, Nixon's alma mater. These citizens did not know about the rejected ultimatum or about DUCK HOOK, both of which were top secret. That Nixon did not carry through with his threats to Hanoi cannot be directly credited to the

Moratorium, but it is clear that the president did not want his carefully structured diplomatic and military moves forced by public pressure.[12]

On 3 November Nixon made one of his most notable public addresses on the war, his nationally televised 'Silent Majority' speech. Outwardly it appeared to be his answer to the Moratorium, and undoubtedly it was in part. With a second moratorium planned for 15 November, the president specifically felt compelled to answer what he alleged was the minority of Americans in the streets calling for what amounted to a US surrender in Vietnam to the 'forces of totalitarianism.' Toward the end of his address, he looked directly into the television camera and made an appeal: 'And so tonight – to you, the great silent majority of my fellow Americans – I ask for your support.'[13] In the days following, the president made additional moves to affect public opinion. The administration announced an additional withdrawal of 60,000 US troops from Vietnam, a cancellation of draft calls for the remainder of the year, and the beginning in December of a Selective Service lottery system that would greatly reduce the number of men exposed to possible military induction. Although the 15 November Moratorium attracted very large crowds in some cities, overall participation was down from October and the momentum for further monthly events ended. Although he had presented no objective evidence that there was a Silent Majority, he had gained some relief from public pressure.

Cast against the secret background of Nixon's Vietnam strategies, the speech took on additional meaning. The administration had abandoned the madman strategy and was putting forward Vietnamization, not as a political move, but as a legitimate way to gain an honorable US exit from Vietnam. In the speech, as delivered, the president declared that there were two choices for the United States in Vietnam. The first was 'immediate, precipitate withdrawal.' He rejected this option without comment and identified the second choice as the 'right way.' That option was to persist in efforts toward a negotiated settlement, but if that proved impossible, to continue 'implementation of our plan for Vietnamization ... in which we will withdraw all our forces from Vietnam on a schedule in accordance with our program, as the South Vietnamese become strong enough to defend their own freedom.' In late September, when Nixon's speech writers first began work on this address, the 1 November deadline and DUCK HOOK represented the current policy. A 27 September draft proclaimed: 'We can slowly withdraw our forces. But let no one call this the way to peace.' Instead, it continued, 'Hanoi's rigidity at the peace table' left only one option: 'Our adversary will not heed our words because he refuses to believe we have the will to use our power. He cannot go on in this delusion. The United States has no choice but to take action to prove to Hanoi that we mean to have an honorable peace in Vietnam.' The draft left a space to insert the DUCK HOOK punitive actions then under consideration.[14] The Silent Majority speech of 3 November, then, began to define 'successful conclusion' and 'honorable peace' not as gaining a political settlement with Hanoi, but as leaving Vietnam with the Saigon regime strong enough to defend itself. This juncture marked the beginning of what would become over time the so-called decent interval strategy that would separate the military with-drawal of US power from whatever final political fate befell the RVN.

Cambodia and Kent State

After a year in office, what had been Johnson's War had become Nixon's War. There had been no quick end of the conflict as the president had asserted he would achieve. There had been no breakthrough in negotia-tions with Hanoi. Despite the attention drawn to Nixon's troop reduc-tions, 475,200 US military personnel still remained in South Vietnam at the end of 1969. During the year, 9414 Americans had been killed in action, a total second only to 1968, which was the bloodiest year of the war for the United States. As an official US Army history of the war observed, the Nixon administration's Vietnamization policy was 'the recognition that the United States could no longer support an open-ended military commitment in Southeast Asia.' 'Americans wanted less, not more, involvement in Vietnam,' the Army historian wrote. General Creighton Abrams, the US commander in Vietnam, would have liked to have been able to bring overwhelming US power to bear on the battle-field, but 'the success of American policy seemed to depend increas-ingly on the actions of the South Vietnamese themselves.'[15]

In an effort to make Vietnamization successful, US aid built the armed forces of the RVN up to about a million soldiers by 1970, and most of its units were armed with the same M-16 automatic rifles and other infantry weapons and artillery pieces available to US forces. Under the leadership of William Colby, the Civilian Operations and Revolutionary Development Support (CORDS) program contributed to Vietnamization through accelerated pacification that included greater village security, identification and capture of Vietcong cadre, and land reform programs. General Abrams shelved William Westmoreland's former emphasis on big-unit operations. The new commander integrated the operations of US forces under the Military Assistance Command,

Vietnam (MACV) into a combined strategy with the Army of the Republic of Vietnam (ARVN) and CORDS to improve population security throughout South Vietnam.

Although Vietnamization had some real successes, old problems and new ones continued to undermine the effort to help the South Vietnamese help themselves. Desertions, unauthorized absences, and unit commanders who listed false names on their unit rosters to pocket pay for these ghost soldiers meant that the actual strength of Saigon's forces was far less than reported. Many ARVN officers and enlisted men lacked the education and training for the high technology weapons and command and control systems provided by the United States. Soldiers' families often lived in or around ARVN camps limiting unit mobility and military effectiveness. Civilian officials regularly falsified village statistics and reports making pacification operations impossible to manage. Tension between US soldiers and the ARVN increased as both were wary of the intentions of the other to fight for a common cause. Among US soldiers in Vietnam, the growing conviction among Americans at home that the war was a mistake was affecting morale. The perception was that the United States was seeking a way out of the war, and for many soldiers individual survival of their tour of duty rather than accomplishment of their unit's mission became their motivation. Disciplinary problems, especially use of marijuana and heroin, increased. Since the United States had not mobilized the nation's manpower for a long war, a shortage of qualified junior officers and experienced noncommissioned officers challenged the institutional ability of the US military to respond to these difficulties.[16]

Despite the dubious progress of Vietnamization, Nixon announced in March 1970 that the plan was proceeding well and US force levels would be reduced by 150,000 in the year ahead. To try to reassure the Saigon government and to strengthen the ARVN, the Nixon administration also continued intensive bombing of the Ho Chi Minh Trail in Laos and enemy sanctuaries in Cambodia. Lavish use of air power provided tactical support of US and ARVN ground operations in South Vietnam, and bombing of surface-to-air missile sites and other military targets in North Vietnam also occurred under the heading of protective reaction strikes. The extent of most of this bombing was kept concealed from the American public, although it was, of course, well known to DRV leaders.[17]

Seeking a 'big play' to counter the diplomatic, military, and public relations frustrations that the war continued to present, Nixon seized upon an opportunity presented when a coup on 18 March 1970 in

Cambodia replaced that country's neutralist leader, Prince Norodom Sihanouk, with a pro-American general, Lon Nol. Enemy use of Cambodian territory along the South Vietnamese border for infiltration and base areas had remained a problem for US and ARVN forces despite the American bombing. The change of regimes in Phnom Penh made it possible to consider a ground sweep across the border with official Cambodian cooperation. More appealing to Nixon than possible military gains was the chance to demonstrate to Hanoi American daring and determination. It was a modification of the madman approach.

On 30 April the president went on national television to announce that, in response to a call for assistance from Cambodia, he had authorized US and South Vietnamese armed forces to launch attacks 'to clean out major enemy sanctuaries on the Cambodian–Viet-Nam border' and to 'attack the headquarters for the entire Communist military operation in South Viet-Nam' that had 'been occupied by the North Vietnamese and Viet Cong for 5 years in blatant violation of Cambodia's neutrality.' He insisted this action was not an invasion but was an incursion of limited duration. Its explicit purpose, he emphasized, was 'to protect our men who are in Viet-Nam and to guarantee the continued success of our withdrawal and Vietnamization programs.' While seeking to reassure the American public that this operation was not escalation but rather part of the de-escalation of American military involvement in Southeast Asia, Nixon also struck a belligerent and defiant tone at the end of the speech:

> If, when the chips are down, the world's most powerful nation, the United States of America, acts like a pitiful, helpless giant, the forces of totalitarianism and anarchy will threaten free nations and free institutions throughout the world. ... I would rather be a one-term President and do what I believe is right than to be a two-term President at the cost of seeing America become a second-rate power and to see this nation accept the first defeat in its proud 190-year history.[18]

Military results of the incursion were modest. American troops were out of Cambodia by the end of June, although some ARVN units remained just inside of Cambodia. Some North Vietnamese supply lines, weapons caches, and small bunker complexes were found and eliminated, and moderate casualties were inflicted on the enemy. The central headquarters for Hanoi's war in the South that Nixon had declared to be a major objective was not discovered. During and after the incursion, however, North Vietnam increased assistance to the Khmer Rouge, the small

Cambodian Communist party that opposed Lon Nol but had always resisted close ties with the Vietnam Communist Party. On the diplomatic front, the DRV used the Cambodian fighting as a reason to break off secret talks that Kissinger had begun with Politburo member Le Duc Tho in Paris on 21 February and to boycott the public peace talks.

On the American domestic front, Nixon had anticipated criticism in the press, in Congress, and on the campuses, but the adverse reaction to his Cambodian 'invasion' – as protesters labeled it – created the greatest domestic crisis he had encountered. Nixon and Kissinger routinely kept policy planning details from Secretary of Defense Laird and Secretary of State William Rogers, whom they treated more as functionaries than policy advisers. When Rogers learned of the Cambodian attack just as it was to be launched, he predicted that it would 'make the students puke.'[19] An angry storm of protests erupted following the president's speech, and demonstrations formed on hundreds of campuses. The administration might have been able to weather this gale, but the reality turned bloody and tragic on the campus of Kent State University in Ohio.

As was happening at many colleges on the weekend of 2–3 May, Kent State was the scene of a rowdy mixture of antiwar activism and springtime partying. In the midst of this turmoil, protesters burned the old wooden structure that housed the Reserve Officer Training Corps (ROTC) program, and some other minor damage occurred in bar and restaurant areas near the campus. The governor of Ohio ordered national guard units to the campus to back up local and state police. By Monday 4 May the weekend excitement had passed, but uniformed soldiers with standard military-issue rifles occupied the school's grounds. At noon a group of a few hundred students gathered in the center of campus near the athletic victory bell to protest the war and the guard's presence. Using tear gas, the soldiers broke up the crowd and followed some of the students down a hill. Inexplicably, some of the soldiers suddenly fired their high-powered rifles toward the dispersing students, killing four and wounding several others. Some of the victims were bystanders or people changing classes and had not even been part of the demonstration. No guardsmen faced criminal charges for their actions, but the state later made a civil settlement with families of the victims.

The killings at Kent State outraged students and the parents of students all over the country. More antiwar demonstrations followed. On hundreds of campuses, boycotts of classes by faculty and students shut down institutions for days. Some universities did not reopen for the remainder of the spring semester. At Jackson State College in Mississippi on 14 May, police shot into a dormitory and killed two students following an antiwar rally, although there were also overtones of racial tensions in this incident. Some citizens argued that criminal acts by demonstrators, such as burning buildings, required authorities to use force, but many other Americans decried the resort to deadly violence. Regardless, the stress of the war on domestic society was clear. Nixon became the target of intense criticism for his Cambodian policies and his insensitivity to the right and protection of free expression. A crowd estimated at more than 75,000 demonstrated on 9 May in the park adjacent to the White House, requiring police to circle the president's home with buses. Nixon later recalled in his memoirs that 'those few days after Kent State were among the darkest of my presidency.'[20] In the wake of the Kent State incident, Nixon announced a definite end of the Cambodian incursion by the first of June and expressed understanding of the idealism that motivated demonstrators. Students soon returned to focusing on the usual pursuits of education and seeking jobs. The experience had been sobering for the president and the protesters, and both sides became more careful about confrontation. US troop reductions continued with only 334,600 in South Vietnam as 1970 ended. Americans killed in action numbered 4221 for the year, less than half the total for 1969.[21]

Stalemate continues

Before the Cambodian incursion interrupted talks, Kissinger had held three fruitless negotiating sessions in Paris with Le Duc Tho, and on 7 September he returned to these secret discussions to try to break the diplomatic stalemate. He presented a 'schedule for total withdrawal' of US forces over 12 months. For the first time in any direct negotiating session, the US position did not couple American withdrawal with an explicit provision for the DRV to remove its forces from the South. Nixon's aide also informed the North Vietnamese that 'we are prepared – I can say this on the highest authority – to have a political contest in *all* of South Vietnam, in areas controlled by the Saigon government as well as in other areas.'[22] This statement and others signaled a new willingness by Washington to link rather than to separate political and military issues. Taken together, these new ideas of possibly leaving PAVN units in the RVN and an open political contest in the South hinted that the United States might not be wedded to an agreement that would ensure the political future of Nguyen Van Thieu. At this particular meeting, Ambassador Xuan Thuy of the DRV would not depart from his government's long-standing insistence that President Thieu and Vice President Nguyen Cao Ky be explicitly excluded from any agreed political process, and Kissinger reaffirmed that the United States would not drop support of them prior to an election.

The affirmation of Vietnamization as US policy in the Silent Majority speech and the president's public defense of the Cambodian incursion as a safeguard of Vietnamization outwardly presented the commitment to the survival and success of an independent South Vietnam as the Nixon administration's goal, just as it had been for Eisenhower, Kennedy, and Johnson. Secretly, however, Nixon and Kissinger were qualifying that commitment. They did not necessarily assume that the Thieu regime would fail, and a total withdrawal of US forces from South Vietnam did not mean that other forms of American assistance could not remain available to Saigon. After almost two decades of US support for the RVN, however, the long-term ability of the Saigon regime to survive on its own remained highly problematical. Hanoi had essentially called the president's bluff when he attempted his madman strategy. Without an escalation of US forces and costs to a level that the American public would never countenance, Washington could not coerce Hanoi into capitulation. Nixon and Kissinger were pragmatists who were shaping an exit strategy to protect their own political interests and with it the image of the United States. They knew they had to end the US military intervention in Vietnam before the 1972 presidential election, and they were not certain whether removal of direct US military leverage on the DRV would mean the end of South Vietnam. They were certain, however, that if Saigon fell into political oblivion, they could not allow it to appear to the American people or to the world that they had pushed it over the edge. As Kissinger wrote privately in July, 'We are ready to withdraw all of our forces by a fixed date and let objective realities shape the political future. ... We want a decent interval.'[23]

Throughout 1971 Nixon continued to tout Vietnamization, but, after the long Americanization of the war, progress was slow. The declining US force level in Vietnam and with it a precipitous decline in both American casualties and monthly draft calls helped the president ease political concerns at home. Washington reduced its troop level to 156,000 by December 1971 and poured aid and matériel into the South. The ARVN became one of the best equipped forces in the world. American planes continued heavy bombardment of supply lines in Laos and Cambodia and air strikes against targets in North Vietnam, including some massive 'limited duration' attacks on fuel depots and anti-aircraft sites.[24] Still, the will and ability of South Vietnamese forces to take charge of the warfare did not improve.

A key test of Vietnamization began on 8 February 1971 when the ARVN launched a major offensive thrust into Laos code named Operation LAM SON 719. The objective was to destroy a major PAVN supply depot at Tchepone and to disrupt North Vietnamese supply lines that passed through Laos. Although officially a neutral nation, Laos had been the scene of a secret war since the early 1960s. The DRV used the sparsely populated country as a route for its Ho Chi Minh Trail that carried vital supplies and reenforcements into South Vietnam. Also, the communist-led Pathet Lao, which waged continuous insurrection against the royal Laotian government, was an ally and, indeed, an appendage of the ruling party in the DRV. In an effort to deny North Vietnam's use of Laotian territory, the United States had dropped thousands of tons of bombs on the Ho Chi Minh Trail and had used the CIA to train and supply the Hmong minority in Laos as a secret army to combat the Pathet Lao. After the reaction to his use of US troops in Cambodia, Nixon did not dare send US forces into Laos with the ARVN, but he authorized heavy American air support of LAM SON 719.

On 6 March the ARVN reached their target of Tchepone, which US bombardment had largely leveled. The 20-mile invasion route had been hotly contested. The 21,000 South Vietnamese soldiers, including elite marine and airborne units, had encountered a similar sized PAVN force that was well equipped with armor and artillery. Having accomplished its mission, the ARVN began withdrawing. Seeing an opportunity to discredit Vietnamization, PAVN commanders then launched a major counterattack with a force of about 36,000 that had been reenforced from the DRV. The ARVN withdrawal under pressure became a debacle. The South Vietnamese lost about 2000 killed in action, and large numbers of tanks, vehicles, artillery, and other equipment were left behind. In the end, LAM SON 719 achieved some benefits for the RVN in possibly forestalling a major PAVN offensive in 1971 and thus giving Saigon more time to strengthen itself before the American departure. Overall the South's armed forces, including some of its best-trained units, had not performed well and had been helped by US air power in avoiding even greater disaster. A facade to provide the Nixon administration an honorable political cover for US withdrawal, Vietnamization offered little hope for future South Vietnamese success in battle.[25]

As Nixon's efforts to build up South Vietnam's own staying power were floundering, domestic opposition to the administration's conduct of the war was growing. From 19 to 23 April, the Vietnam Veterans Against the War (VVAW) staged a dramatic protest event called Operation DEWEY CANYON III. During a week of rallies and political theater in Washington, several hundred veterans conducted what they described as 'a limited incursion into the country of Congress.' A high point came when many of them tossed their combat medals and ribbons across a police barricade and onto the steps of the Capitol. The day before, a former Navy Lieutenant with several combat decorations, John Kerry of Massachusetts, appeared before a Senate hearing as a spokesman for the VVAW. His words were angry and bitter:

> I want to relate to you the feeling that many of the men who have returned to this country express because we are probably angriest about all that we were told about Vietnam and about the mystical war against communism. ... Now we are told that the men who fought there must watch quietly while American lives are lost so that we can exercise the incredible arrogance of Vietnamizing the Vietnamese.
>
> Each day to facilitate the process by which the United States washes her hands of Vietnam someone has to give up his life so that the United States doesn't have to admit something that the entire world already knows, so that we can't say that we have made a mistake. Someone has to die so that President Nixon won't be, and these are his words, 'the first President to lose a war.'
>
> We are asking Americans to think about that because how do you ask a man to be the last man to die in Vietnam? How do you ask a man to be the last man to die for a mistake?[26]

In addition to the unsettling message of warriors protesting their own war, the nation wrestled with news accounts of the trial of Lieutenant William Calley, whom a court martial found guilty in April 1971 of the murder of 'at least 22' noncombatants in the 1968 massacre of the entire village of My Lai by American soldiers. A poll revealed that 91 percent of those asked had followed the trial closely and that the respondents were almost equally divided between those who agreed with the verdict, disagreed, and were undecided. The differences in their opinions came from whether they thought blame could be placed on one young man for his part in this atrocity or whether the crime was the war itself. For most observers, the evidence presented about the murders made even clearer what a liability the war had become to America's self-image and self-confidence.[27]

Adding to the domestic debate on the war, the *New York Times* began publishing on 13 June a series of articles based upon a secret history of Vietnam War decisions through 1967 prepared by the Department of Defense. What became known as the Pentagon Papers was 7000 pages of narrative and documents intended for internal government use that had been surreptitiously photocopied by Daniel Ellsberg, a Defense Department official, and leaked to the media. Having become disillusioned like Kerry and members of the VVAW, Ellsberg was a former marine and erstwhile supporter of US intervention in Vietnam who came to be strongly opposed to continued US involvement, he leaked the documents to show, as in fact they did, that many of the critical decisions that had led to a major war were ill considered and often influenced by the domestic political interests of US leaders rather than any understanding of military, political, and social realities in Vietnam.

The pugnacious Nixon considered all of these criticisms threats to his leadership. He fought back fiercely. He had the Justice Department seek court injunctions against the VVAW's DEWEY CANYON III, and members of his staff attempted to attack the reputation and credibility of John Kerry. Nixon personally intervened in Calley's case by ordering him released from prison and announcing he would review the court's decision, much to the dismay of military prosecutors who were trying to protect the beleaguered reputation of the US military by bringing a mass murderer to justice. The leak of the Pentagon Papers especially enraged Nixon and Kissinger. They obtained an unprecedented court order to stop newspaper publication of the documents, but the Supreme Court vacated this so-called prior restraint on press freedom and allowed publication. Leaks were so offensive to the secrecy that Nixon demanded, however, that the White House then began its own illegal efforts to harass Ellsberg, whom Kissinger termed 'the most dangerous man in America today.' Convinced that there was a conspiracy of political opponents seeking to destroy him, Nixon created a group of White House operatives, known as the 'plumbers,' whose job it was to find and stop leaks of information. It was some of these plumbers who would in 1972 break into the Watergate office building and set off a chain of events that would destroy Nixon's presidency.[28]

The narrowing of US military options in Vietnam and the widening domestic dissent on the war put ever greater pressure on the administration to advance the negotiations with Hanoi. Kissinger labored secretly to gain a face-saving diplomatic formula for the United States. On 31 May 1971, he made a significant offer to remove US troops six months after an agreement was signed for a cease-fire was in place. This formulation represented a unilateral American withdrawal that would leave

DRV troops in the South. It set as conditions that Hanoi would end infiltrations of its forces into the South and would release US prisoners of war (POWs). The proposal also included the idea that political issues in South Vietnam would be left to the Vietnamese to resolve. Kissinger later labeled this demarche 'a turning point in our diplomacy in Vietnam' because it set the basic outlines for the agreement ultimately signed in 1973.[29]

Le Duc Tho countered on 26 June with language that also marked a shift in the DRV's previously hardline position. Tho accepted the cease-fire idea and agreed to a prisoner release, but he called for the United States to stop air attacks against North Vietnam, pay war reparations, and not support Thieu in elections scheduled in the RVN for the fall. The significant change in Hanoi's position was that it did not demand the removal of Thieu and other specific South Vietnamese leaders as a precondition for a cease-fire. Both sides were reassessing their positions. The fighting in Laos had exposed the weakness of Vietnamization and had encouraged the PAVN, but it had also cost the North heavy casualties and delayed for probably a year its ability to launch its own offensive. Nixon was feeling domestic pressure as the 1972 presidential election grew closer, but Hanoi was getting pressure from its major suppliers in China and the USSR to be more flexible in its diplomatic stance. After some real discussion of terms over several meetings, ultimately neither side rejected or accepted the other's proposals. The impasse remained as both sides continued to fight while talking. Hanoi believed that the US terms would still give an advantage to Thieu over the Provisional Revolutionary Government (PRG), which was the political organization of the NLF. Conversely, Washington reasoned that more time would allow Vietnamization and air power to reduce 'the risk of South Vietnam crumbling around our remaining forces.' As Kissinger put it to Nixon in September 1971, 'We could heal the wounds in this country as our men left peace behind on the battlefield and a healthy interval for South Vietnam's fate to unfold.'[30]

The Paris agreement to end the war

In the fall of 1971 a diplomatic agreement to end the war remained derailed by the specific issue of the fate of Nguyen Van Thieu. In the public talks in Paris, Hanoi's representatives had declared a willingness to accept the outcome of the approaching presidential voting in South Vietnam, if it were indeed a free election. It was evident that the DRV and PRG anticipated that Thieu would lose, and the Nixon administration chose to represent their position as another demand for Thieu's removal. Initially the principal candidates were Thieu, Vice President Nguyen Cao Ky, and General Duong Van Minh, who had led the 1963 coup against Ngo Dinh Diem and favored talks with the PRG. This three-way race created the possibility that Minh might win if the other two split the pro-government vote. US officials continued both to announce publicly their support of the RVN president and to provide secretly the funds to bribe South Vietnamese legislators, who voted to disqualify Ky from the contest. With Ky out of the race, the US Embassy thought that the presence of Minh on the ballot would preserve an appearance of democracy but not threaten Thieu's reelection. Before election day, however, Minh withdrew rather than lend legitimacy to the US plan, and Ky rejected a last minute legal maneuver by the RVN courts to put his name back on the ballot. Thieu swept to victory on 3 October with 94.3 percent of the vote. A North Vietnamese diplomat later reflected that the Nixon administration sought to maintain the Saigon government and exclude the PRG: 'We [saw] that they would like to have all the cake.'[31]

During the first half of 1972, both the United States and DRV made their own big plays to end the American war in Vietnam. For his part, Nixon went on a global diplomatic offensive. In February 1972 he made a turning-point visit to the People's Republic of China (PRC) that reversed over 20 years of American refusal to communicate with Beijing. In May 1972 Nixon traveled to Moscow and signed a nuclear arms limitation agreement with the Soviet Union. Although much tension remained in US–China and US–Soviet relations, these diplomatic breakthroughs took some of the danger out of the Cold War concerns that were at the foundation of the US presence in Vietnam. On the other hand, Nixon's hopes that Moscow and Beijing would urge Hanoi to compromise were not realized.

America's triangular diplomacy brought back to North Vietnamese leaders unpleasant reminders of the Geneva Conference of 1954 when neither of their socialist allies had been willing to risk their own national interests to insist on a final political settlement in Vietnam. While in Beijing, Nixon asked directly for PRC endorsement of a negotiated settlement in Indochina. Chinese Prime Minister Zhou Enlai responded firmly that 'so long as the Vietnamese, the Laos, and Cambodians continue to fight, we will not stop supporting them for a single day,' and Zhou sent a copy of this statement to Hanoi. When Nixon and Zhou issued a joint communiqué on their talks, it declared their agreement on opposition to the efforts of any country to establish 'hegemony' in the Asia–Pacific region. This language was an obvious reference to the Soviet Union. Later in Moscow, Nixon asked Soviet leaders to back compromise in Vietnam, but they, too, indicated that they would go on supplying North Vietnam. Despite reassurances from both Beijing and Moscow of continued support, Hanoi was unconvinced. The Vietnamese interpreted both summits to mean that the USSR and PRC valued good relations with the United States enough to qualify their backing of the DRV. As a Communist Party officer in Hanoi told a Japanese journalist, 'sometimes dealings between big nations may be made at the expense of a small nation and crush it.'[32]

Nixon's strong support for Thieu in the RVN elections and his hand-shake with China's supreme leader Mao Zedong in Beijing, seen world-wide in newspaper photographs, demonstrated to strategists in Hanoi that they needed to continue military pressure on South Vietnam to gain the balance of force required for a negotiated settlement they could accept. Vietnamization meant that the United States continued to flood the South with military matériel, but it also meant that US troop levels were dropping below 100,000 and that those remaining Americans were mostly in noncombat units. Consequently, on 30 March 1972, the PAVN launched a three-pronged strategic offensive. Quickly dubbed the Easter Offensive by journalists, it was directed against provincial capitals and ARVN bases in northern South Vietnam, the Central Highlands, and along the Cambodian border north of Saigon.

These assaults inflicted heavy losses on ARVN units, and the US command responded with ferocious air strikes against the attackers including use of B-52 heavy bombers. Nixon was angry with Hanoi, but also with Moscow for not restraining its ally. He was also fearful that a total collapse of the RVN could severely damage him in the upcoming presidential election. In an operation code named LINEBACKER, Nixon authorized large-scale bombing of the logistics lines in the north-ern part of the DRV and the mining of Haiphong Harbor. Since Soviet ships off-loaded at Haiphong, this move put the announced US–USSR summit at risk, but Moscow placed a high premium on détente with Washington, especially in response to Nixon's courting of the Chinese leaders. The Kremlin allowed the summit to proceed. The Easter Offensive lasted for three months, but failed to topple the Saigon government. The communist forces had to withdraw from some gains, such as possession of Quang Tri City. The assault resulted in some new PAVN territorial control along the RVN border with Cambodia and addi-tional PRG influence in the delta. Although some ARVN units performed well, overall the fighting again demonstrated the flaws in Vietnamization. American military advisers and US bombing were decisive factors in many battles. Hanoi discovered that, although diminished, US firepower was still dangerous and that the PAVN was not strong enough to coerce the United States into a settlement.

Neither the United States nor North Vietnam had gained the negotiating advantage that it sought, and thus both returned to the bargaining table. In October 1972 Kissinger and Le Duc Tho discussed a cease-fire in place, return of US POWs, temporary continuation of Thieu's government in office, and permission for PAVN units to remain in the South. Although the language appeared to contain significant concessions by both sides, a tentative agreement emerged in which it was the United States that had moved farthest. Upon implementation of the terms, US ground and air forces would be completely withdrawn, and the PAVN would remain in the South to face the RVN's notoriously ineffective forces. After Kissinger briefed Thieu on the terms, the RVN president strongly protested US disregard for its Saigon ally. The governments in both Hanoi and Saigon publicized parts of the agreement in competing efforts to influence Washington. Embarrassed by these leaks and disappointed by Thieu's obstructionism, Kissinger on 26 October declared to the press that 'peace was at hand' but some details remained to be decided. Although Nixon had authorized Kissinger to make the concessions leading to the tentative agreement, the president now decided to delay its acceptance. He and his aide knew that the United States was on the verge of getting out of Vietnam – the last US combat unit had left Vietnam in August – but they refused to abandon Thieu outright. It would be politically damaging on the eve of the November election to appear to run out on an ally, something they had been accusing their political opponents of advocating. They also still believed they could depart the war in a way that would leave the Saigon government a decent interval of time after that departure to try to make it on its own.[33]

On 7 November, Nixon won reelection as president in a landslide victory over Democratic, antiwar candidate Senator George McGovern. The senator was an early and vocal congressional critic of the war. He had cosponsored with Senator Mark Hatfield an unsuccessful Senate resolution calling on Nixon to withdraw all US forces from Vietnam. After gaining his party's nomination for president, he had met in September in Paris and Saigon with North and South Vietnamese officials. Publicly he characterized the massive US military intervention in Vietnam as a mistake, and privately he tried to get Hanoi to agree to release to him a list of all US POWs, which the DRV had been withholding from US diplomats. North Vietnamese leaders welcomed McGovern's challenge to Nixon, but they found his specific proposals simplistic and would not offer him anything that they had not conceded already. Although most of the American electorate wanted the US involvement in Vietnam to end, the Nixon campaign was able to portray McGovern's unilateral withdrawal proposals as radical policies with dangerous consequences for American security. Kissinger's 'peace was at hand' comment only days before the election had some impact on the vote, although journalists who speculated that it was a crass political ploy did not know how close the negotiators were to agreement. Also, the Democrats could not get voters to question Nixon's fitness for office on the basis of news stories revealing the participation of White House staff members in a June burglary of the Democratic National Headquarters in Washington's Watergate hotel-office building. The president won 60.7 percent of the popular vote and all but 17 electoral votes.[34]

In the days after the election, Kissinger and Tho resumed talks. Thieu remained the obstacle, and the US side introduced what Kissinger later labeled 'preposterous' revisions to try to gain his acquiescence. These new terms placed significant restrictions on the PAVN and PRG. The United States also began Operation ENHANCE PLUS, which provided the ARVN with thousands of pieces of heavy military equipment: tanks, airplanes, helicopters, and artillery pieces. Nixon sent Thieu letters of personal assurance that American technical assistance would be available to his forces even after US troops were gone and that American B-52 attacks would be used if the DRV threatened to overwhelm his forces. Hanoi did not know the terms of these secret offers, but in early December it made a tough response to Kissinger's new treaty provisions by withdrawing some of its earlier concessions and making new firm demands of its own. When the talks recessed on 13 December for the Christmas holidays, Kissinger was very frustrated by both the DRV and RVN. He reported to Nixon that 'Hanoi is almost disdainful of us because we have no effective leverage left, while Saigon in its short-sighted devices to sabotage the agreement knocks out from under us our few remaining props.'[35] The way out of this dilemma, he suggested, was either to turn on the DRV with bombing or resume talks in January while still trying to entice agreement from Thieu.

Nixon chose the first option in what became Operation LINE-BACKER II or the Christmas Bombing, as journalists called it. From 18 to 29 December, US aircraft, many of them B-52s, dropped 20,000 tons of high explosives on North Vietnam, including some targets near Hanoi that resulted in 'collateral' or incidental damage in Hanoi. It was the most concentrated bombing of the entire war, and the president intended it to intimidate the DRV and to impress Thieu with US resolve. It was a strategy that revived Nixon's old madman theory and combined it with the effort he and Kissinger had pursued for two years to fashion an end to the intervention that left Saigon with a chance for political survival. After a White House dinner on the evening the Christmas Bombing began, the president told a dinner guest that 'he did not care if the whole world thought he was crazy. ... If it did, so much the better; the Russians and Chinese might think they were dealing with a madman and so had better force North Vietnam into a settlement before the world was consumed in a larger war.'[36]

On 8 January Kissinger and Tho resumed talks in Paris and made rapid progress toward settlement. Advocates of strategic bombing at that time and later declared that concentrated US bombing like LINE-BACKER II should have been used earlier and more often and would have produced a favorable result in the war with much less cost to the United States. This conclusion is highly dubious. Tho had agreed to resume talks before the bombing began. Furthermore, the DRV had endured the bombing quite well and had inflicted heavy losses on the attackers. In what Hanoi called 'Twelve Days of Dienbienphu in the Air,' the North's missiles, antiaircraft artillery, and MiG interceptors had downed 13 tactical bombers and 15 of the B-52 strategic bombers (12 percent of the big bombers deployed in the raids) with corresponding losses of the air crews. Most notable, the goal of the bombing was to get Hanoi to agree to what it had already agreed to in October and to what was a compromise settlement very different from what could be termed military victory. The evidence indicates that Thieu was the obstacle in October and that the bombing was for his benefit. After the bombing stopped and talks were ready to resume, Nixon gave Thieu a personal, secret promise that the United States would respond with 'full force' similar to LINEBACKER II to any DRV violations of a signed agreement.[37]

On 27 January 1973, the United States, DRV, RVN, and the PRG signed in Paris the Agreement Ending the War and Restoring Peace in Vietnam. Its terms were virtually identical to those that Kissinger and Tho had drafted in October. It provided for a cease-fire with PAVN and ARVN forces remaining in place, but did not specify precisely where those forces were located. All US and other foreign troops were to be out of Vietnam within 60 days, and during that same period US prisoners of war would be released. The RVN and PRG were to create a National

Council of National Reconciliation and Concord to supervise compliance with the agreements and to prepare for elections and reunification through 'peaceful means.'[38] The only terms of this document that were fulfilled were the withdrawal of the 23,000 US troops in Vietnam and the release of 591 American POWs from North Vietnamese jails. There was no meaningful cease-fire, no delineation of who controlled what territory, no council of reconciliation, no elections, and no peaceful reunification. Nixon declared that his announced goal of peace with honor had been realized because the Thieu government remained in place in Saigon. How long, and for what interval, that regime might survive he did not predict.

6

Conclusions: Peace at Last and Lasting Legacies

Richard Nixon's compromise peace finally ended the futile quest of over 25 years to find an American solution for Vietnam's post-colonial political and social structure. The departure of the last American troops left the outcome to be decided by the Vietnamese themselves. Nixon maintained that the 1973 accord was peace with honor, because US forces departed with the Republic of Vietnam (RVN) government still in place and well-stocked with US arms. Although Kissinger claimed to support Nixon's assessment, he made other comments suggesting more cynically that the diplomatic settlement provided a decent interval between the end of US operations and the final political resolution. During that interval Nixon resigned the presidency in the face of impeachment charges connected to the cover-up of Watergate-related crimes. For US policy in Vietnam, the end came on 30 April 1975 when US helicopters lifted the last remaining US personnel from the roof of the American embassy as the People's Army of Vietnam (PAVN) occupied the RVN government buildings in Saigon.[1]

The United States renewed its commitment in Vietnam year after year because of concern about the credibility and consequences for US policy outside Vietnam. Successive American leaders worried about how American strength and reliability was being perceived in friendly and hostile capitals around the world and among Americans themselves. With the international order framed by hostile US and Soviet rhetoric and the US and Chinese clash in Korea still echoing throughout Asia, some cautious intervention by the United States in Vietnam was understandable and even prudent after the Geneva Conference. Despite US economic and military power, however, Washington's ability to shape the domestic structure of Vietnam was always limited. US policy moved from counterinsurgency, to combat, and finally to compromise; but it never was able to translate American power and good intentions into political viability in Saigon. In fact, as the US war in Vietnam grew to excessive proportions, any credibility of the RVN as an independent state vanished and the danger of direct American conflict with China and the USSR increased.

Despite the apocalyptic rhetoric of the Truman Doctrine and the domino theory, the Vietnam War was always a limited war for the United States. For the Vietnamese, on the contrary, it was a total war. Their lives and futures were at complete risk. In the political and economic interconnections of the twentieth-century world, a powerful nation like the United States could not leave events in any region entirely beyond its notice and influence. Washington, however, lost its sense of proportion. What should have been a modest American interest in Southeast Asia became major. American leaders tended to think of the conflict in absolute terms of all or nothing. After the war, Americans continued to debate the idea of 'no more Vietnams.' For some that negative adage meant no US intervention anywhere, and for others it meant no more limited, losing interventions anywhere. Experience showed, however, that both notions were faulty. The United States was a nation among nations, and it could neither avoid nor dominate the world around it.

Brother enemies

At the end of January 1973 the American War in Vietnam formally ended with the signing of the Paris agreement, and the conflict became one of Vietnamese against Vietnamese. Through the centuries, Vietnamese had fought each other many times over land and local power not ideologies, but since 1945 these 'brother enemies,' as each side referred to its Vietnamese adversaries, had been pitted against each other as part of a global ideological contest. This Cold War struggle had always included Vietnamese personalities and indigenous historical identities, but it had also produced two regimes, the RVN and the Democratic Republic of Vietnam (DRV), whose armed forces had been equipped and trained by the United States on one side and the Soviet Union and the People's Republic of China (PRC) on the other. Although there had been a significant number of Soviet and Chinese advisors and support troops in North Vietnam during the war, those nations had not deployed combat divisions in Indochina as the United States had done. External assistance to the competing Vietnamese regimes could be expected to continue, but the fighting itself would be conducted by the PAVN and the Army of the Republic of Vietnam (ARVN).

The 24,000 US troops in South Vietnam at the time of the peace agreement were withdrawn in four groups at 15-day intervals to coordinate with DRV compliance with its pledge to release US prisoners held in the North. The Vietnamese released the first 115 POWs in Hanoi on 12 February, and by 29 March 591 prisoners had been repatriated. These men had endured a difficult captivity, some of them for several years and some of them tortured in efforts to force confessions of aggression and crimes to be used for propaganda. Since a negotiated withdrawal from a stalemated war did not lend itself to victory parades, the safe return of these heroic Americans, mostly air force and navy pilots, provided a rare opportunity for celebration at the military bases and towns that received them back. Their celebrity treatment, which included a White House banquet hosted by President Nixon, contrasted dramatically with the experiences of the tens of thousands of American soldiers who had returned from their year-long tours of duty during the war mostly with no fanfare or even public notice. On 30 March, the last US troops stationed in Saigon, a group of 5200, departed. At the peak of the US deployment in April 1969 there had been 543,400 American military personnel in the South. By terms of the Paris agreement, in April 1973 there were 159 US Marine guards at the US embassy and another 50 US military personnel assigned to the embassy's Defense Attaché Office (DAO).[2]

Although the US ground and air forces had been removed from Vietnam, the RVN's military position seemed strong. The Saigon government claimed to control 75 percent of the land and 85 percent of the population of South Vietnam. Despite the cease-fire, President Thieu ordered his forces to move quickly after the Paris signing to secure disputed territory. Conversely the PAVN chose to conserve its strength, which had been drained by the heavy fighting of the Easter Offensive and the two LINEBACKER operations. North Vietnamese forces in the South and the People's Liberation Armed Forces (PLAF) of the National Liberation Front (NLF) were short on men and supplies. They avoided major combat and worked on replenishing their fighting ability. Despite the terms of the peace agreement, Hanoi infiltrated 140,000 tons of matériel and 100,000 men, including two infantry divisions and several combat regiments, into South Vietnam during 1973.

As the DRV built a logistics network in the South (including roads and pipelines) and consolidated its political strength in some areas, such as the Mekong Delta, the Thieu government's flaws and chronic weaknesses severely limited its long-term prospects for survival. Saigon claimed to control many areas in which local distrust of the government and sympathy with the NLF was strong. Much of the South's military officer corps was hopelessly corrupt. They had gained their positions through bribery and lived well through many forms of extortion. Thieu himself lived in luxury and cemented the loyalty of his top officers through organized corruption. The disappearance of the once sprawling US military bases in South Vietnam increased the unemployment level, which was already high because of the large number of refugees from combat areas. A skyrocketing inflation added to the economic stress. Economic necessity fueled a lively black market in American supplied military and consumer goods that ended up in the hands of the PLAF and PAVN in the RVN. All of these factors steadily weakened the ARVN, and Thieu further increased the vulnerability of his forces by thinly spreading them to try to assert his regime's control over more areas.[3]

Despite Nixon's private assurances to Thieu prior to the signing of the Paris agreement, the administration took no retaliatory military action as the DRV reenforced its forces in the South. In yet another secret maneuver, Nixon had held out the promise to Hanoi of reconstruction aid, and he now tried unsuccessfully to slow Hanoi's resupply efforts by threatening to withhold that assistance. The White House hesitated to order bombing of the infiltration routes because not all of the US prisoners had been released. When the final group was freed at the end of March, Nixon and Kissinger were weighing the possibility of air strikes, using the justification that Hanoi was violating the agreement. They knew there would be a public outcry, but, with the president now safely in a second term, they thought they could withstand public controversy over another big play. As they made these political calculations, the domestic environment of the administration took a dramatic turn.

On 23 March, seven men, who had been convicted for participation in the Watergate burglary, appeared before Judge John J. 'Maximum John' Sirica for sentencing. All faced the threat of long imprisonments, and one of them, seeking to gain leniency, had revealed to the judge that other individuals besides those on trial, and also connected to the White House, were involved. Sirica encouraged the other defendants to talk, and the White House-directed cover-up of illegal activity began to become unraveled. In later years, Nixon and Kissinger both claimed that the Watergate investigations over the next year and a half denied to them the political base to enforce the Paris agreements. It became their contention that it was Congress and the administration's critics that caused the eventual downfall of the RVN by gradually cutting off US support to Saigon. What Nixon and Kissinger might have done without the Watergate hearings and trials cannot be known. What is known is that the White House's own irresponsible actions had created the Watergate issue and that, separate from Watergate, Congress and the public had already made clear their desire to distance the United States from any further risks and costs in support of the Saigon government.

The American-style high technology warfare for which the United States had prepared the RVN armed forces required an expenditure of about $3 billion a year to maintain. In the fiscal year ending 1 July 1973, US military aid had already declined to $2.27 billion as the last US forces withdrew, and that level of assistance continued to decline down to $1.01 billion for the following fiscal year. The ARVN began to experience fuel and munitions shortages. The political will in Congress to fund the fighting was eroding significantly. On 10 May 1973 Congress voted to cut off all funds for the air war in Cambodia – the one remaining 'stick' the US had. A different legislative act in the fall prohibited any US funds from being used to help rebuild North Vietnam – the 'carrot' – as long as Hanoi refused, as it was doing, to account for all Americans missing in action (MIA). On 7 November 1973 Congress passed, over Nixon's veto, the War Powers Resolution that made clear how much the people's representatives disapproved of the way Nixon and his White House predecessors had fashioned the US military intervention in Vietnam. This act required any president to notify Congress within 48 hours of any deployment of US forces into actual or possible combat abroad and to terminate that deployment within 60 days unless there was a formal declaration of war or other formal congressional authorization. Congress had challenged the presidential practice, begun by Harry Truman in Korea, of asserting constitutional authority as commander in chief of the armed forces to conduct war without congressional approval.[4]

A fascinating historical question has developed over what strategy, if any, the Nixon administration had for Vietnam after the Paris agreements. In their memoirs and other writings, Nixon and Kissinger asserted that the peace settlement would have enabled South Vietnam to survive if North Vietnam had observed the cease-fire and other treaty provisions. It was the fault of Congress, not the White House, they further contend, that Hanoi was able to reenforce its troops in the South without any consequences. It was clear as early as the fall of 1969, however, that Nixon and Kissinger's only real strategy had been a phased US withdrawal, not a plan for the RVN's long-term survival.

Their efforts to construct a decent interval of survival for the Saigon regime after the US departure was primarily to limit negative consequences to Nixon's domestic political position and America's international credibility. Nixon, in particular, may have thought that the Thieu government had a real chance to survive. In case it did not, however, as historian Jeffrey Kimball has shown, he and his spokespersons began an immediate public relations campaign to create the image that Nixon had won an honorable peace through firmness and that any blame for failure was on the weakness of others, particularly Congress. Political scientist Larry Berman has taken the evidence a step further to argue that Nixon's secret assurances to Thieu indicated that the strategy was not a decent interval but a plan concealed from the war-weary American public to reenter the war with US air power and sustain Saigon indefinitely.[5]

Whatever his plan, Nixon was never able to follow it because his presidency became paralyzed and then destroyed by the Watergate scandal. Through the first half of 1973, investigative reporters, congressional committees, and special criminal prosecutors probed for evidence of White House, including presidential, involvement in illegal activities. In July the revelation of secret White House tape recordings presented the possibility of exposing the role Nixon himself had in covering up the crimes, as his former aide John Dean had been claiming in public testimony. While investigators fought for months to gain access to the tapes, a separate case of bribery and conspiracy forced the resignation of Vice President Spiro Agnew, and Nixon appointed Congressman Gerald R. Ford as the new vice president. Finally, after many legal maneuvers, the US Supreme Court ruled unanimously that Nixon must surrender subpoenaed tapes to Judge Sirica. Among these recordings was one containing clear evidence that the president had conspired to obstruct justice, a felony offense, when he ordered the CIA to interfere with FBI investigation of the Watergate burglary. Facing certain impeachment and trial, Nixon resigned the presidency on 9 August 1974, and Ford became president. Kissinger remained in the administration in the dual role of national security adviser and secretary of state.[6]

As a member of the Republican leadership in Congress, Ford had supported the decisions of Kennedy and Johnson to provide military support to South Vietnam, but he had criticized Johnson for 'pulling our best punches in Vietnam' and had urged 'maximum use of American conventional air and sea power.' With Nixon's entry into the White House in 1969, Ford had changed his rhetoric to endorse his party's chief executive and praised Nixon's peace with honor goal and the Vietnamization emphasis that 'is bringing Americans home.' When he himself assumed the nation's highest office, Ford understood the political reality that the majority of US citizens demanded not victory in Vietnam but release from the burden of the conflict. In a gesture to ease some of the domestic pain of the war, he announced a conditional amnesty for men accused of draft evasion or military desertion, but, with many war critics still wary of reprisals, only about 6 percent of eligible offenders responded.

Ford remained convinced, however, that US security interests still justified material support of the RVN. The day after taking office, he promised Thieu that previous US commitments 'are still valid and will be fully honored.' He was not aware until months later of Nixon's secret 'respond with full force' pledge to Thieu, but Ford did try to persuade his former congressional colleagues to maintain US aid to Saigon at a level of at least $1 billion. At one point he even threatened to veto legislation that did not provide that amount of aid, but in December he signed an appropriation of only $700 million. The legislators were reflecting the public mood that the seemingly endless American support of South Vietnam would soon have to end.[7] To Ambassador Bui Diem, the RVN's representative in the United States and a man of dignity and character, the disengagement steps of American administrators and legislators both were shameful and unbecoming of a great nation. The decisions were based upon American self-interest with 'callous disregard of the consequences their actions would have on a nation of twenty million people,' the ambassador charged, 'and they did so although it was no longer a matter of American blood, but only of some hundreds of millions of dollars.'[8]

Hanoi had at first been concerned that the United States might reenter the war, especially with bombing. The lack of US response to PAVN infiltration in 1973 and the internal political preoccupation of the American leaders in 1974 convinced Northern leaders that there was little congressional support for renewing US military action. The steady decline in US aid was producing serious shortages of fuel, munitions, and spare parts in the South, and forcing the ARVN into what PAVN officers reported was a 'poor man's war.' On 30 September 1974, the Politburo concluded that even if the United States reentered the fighting it could not reverse the RVN's outlook. To test this proposition the communist forces attacked the lightly guarded and relatively isolated provincial capital of Phuoc Long in mid-December. There were no US air strikes and no ARVN reenforcements sent to the area, and the town and province were under PAVN control by early January. The DRV's prime minister, Pham Van Dong, assured the Politburo that there was no way the Americans would send troops and that even US air and naval forces would no longer be decisive. 'I'm kidding, but also telling the truth,' he remarked, 'when I say that the Americans would not come back even if you offered them candy.'[9] Confident of success, although it might require two more years, Northern leaders approved a major offensive to begin in the spring with an attack against Ban Me Thuot in the Central Highlands.

On 10 March 1975, as a recalcitrant Congress debated a White House request for supplemental aid for SouthVietnam and Cambodia to restore funds cut in late 1974, the PAVN launched its surprise assault on Ban Me Thuot. In a bitter coincidence, the congressional Democrats caucused and voted to oppose any further US funds for Indochina at the same moment as the town was falling into enemy hands. One South Vietnamese official described the announcement of the vote 'like a kick in the groin, deep and painful.'[10] To consolidate his dispersed forces and to better defend the heavily populated coastal areas, Thieu ordered a strategic retreat of the ARVN eastward from the Central Highlands. Although the plan was reasonable in theory, the execution of it was terrible. It allowed the communist forces to walk into the key towns of Pleiku and Kontum, and the redeployment itself turned into a disorderly rout. Military commanders in Hanoi then committed reserve forces to northern South Vietnam targeting the cities of Danang and Hue. The coastal roads became choked with panicked civilians and ARVN soldiers retreating, or more precisely fleeing, southward. By 30 March the PAVN had occupied Hue and Danang, and DRV leaders proclaimed the launching of the Ho Chi Minh Campaign to liberate Saigon and all of South Vietnam from Thieu's puppet regime.

It took the PAVN only four weeks in what had become a conventional invasion operation to mop up the ARVN and seize the southern capital. As the northern troops advanced, Ford went before Congress with a televised speech on 10 April. He boldly requested almost a billion dollars in military and economic aid for South Vietnam to help him 'keep America's word good throughout the world.' He was returning once again to the shopworn notion of credibility, but he changed few minds on Capitol Hill and failed to obtain the supplementary funds he sought. The majority in Congress and among the public had grown tired of the high price of support of Saigon and frankly doubted whether any amount of further financial assistance would alter the outcome. The PAVN juggernaut proceeded toward the RVN capital, although not entirely without resistance. The 18th ARVN Division put up a surprisingly fierce resistance at Xuan Loc, about 50 kilometers east of Saigon, that delayed the enemy advance for two weeks. The ARVN evacuated Xuan Loc on 22 April, and, the next day in a carefully worded phrase in a speech at Tulane University, Ford began to put the war in the past tense. The surprised student audience reacted with extended applause when the president declared that the United States should look ahead because restoring its lost pride 'cannot be achieved by refighting a war that is finished as far as America is concerned.'[11]

The fall of Saigon itself came quickly in the last days of April. On the 21st, Thieu resigned, blaming the United States for abandoning Vietnam. By the 27th, PAVN forces had Saigon completely encircled, and the next day General Duong Van Minh became the RVN's last president. Considered a 'third force' option – he had led the coup against Ngo Dinh Diem in 1963 and had opposed Thieu prior to the 1971 elections – Minh seemed the best choice among southern leaders to negotiate a surrender. The last US ambassador in Saigon, Graham Martin, had resisted preparations for evacuating Americans working in the US embassy because he had not wanted to panic an already frightened Saigon citizenry and, to some degree, had refused to admit the inevitable. When reports reached Washington on 28 April, however, that flight operations were no longer possible at Saigon's Ton Son Nhut airport, Ford ordered the evacuation to begin. Throughout the day on 29 April and into the early morning hours of 30 April, US military helicopters carried about 1000 Americans and 5500 Vietnamese closely connected with the Americans to US Navy ships off the coast. Dramatically and tragically, the helicopters lifted people off of roof tops as thousands of Vietnamese clamored below in futile attempts to join the exodus. Shortly before noon on 30 April, a North Vietnamese T-54 tank crashed through the gates of the presidential palace. President Minh and his staff surrendered unconditionally to Colonel Bui Tin of the PAVN. The victors renamed Saigon 'Ho Chi Minh City.' The 30-year war within Vietnam was over, but the effects of the war would long remain.

Vietnam, Cambodia, and Laos after the war

As the war in Vietnam came to an end, the military conflicts in neighboring Laos and Cambodia also reached a turning-point. Despite their officially neutral standing through much of the Indochina wars, these two kingdoms had been directly impacted by the large struggle in Vietnam. Not only was Laos the location of the DRV's vital supply line – the Ho Chi Minh Trail – but the Laotian Communist Party, the Pathet

Lao, had always been closely connected to Hanoi. As the struggle in Southeast Asia had lengthened, Washington and Hanoi, for many of the same reasons as they negotiated the Paris agreement on Vietnam, pressed the Pathet Lao and the Royal Laotian Government of Prince Souvanna Phouma to negotiate. On 21 February 1973, the Vientiane government and the Lao Patriotic Forces (LPF), as the Pathet Lao styled themselves, signed an 'Agreement to Restore Peace and Reconciliation in Laos.' Paralleling the Vietnam accords, this document left the stronger LPF in possession of key territory, and the government, under pressure from Washington, had acquiesced. With the communist victory in Vietnam in April 1975, the LPF simply took direct possession of government power in Laos. Once in control, the new government turned on the Hmong people who had aided the United States against the communists. The LPF killed thousands of their old enemies, although about 100,000 Hmong managed to migrate to America.[12]

The plight of the Hmong was tragic, but the events that unfolded in Cambodia in 1975 and after were even more horrific. Although Prince Norodom Sihanouk, who headed the Cambodian government after 1954, tried to keep his weak country neutral in the Vietnam War, the PAVN's use of eastern Cambodia as a supply and base area for its operations in South Vietnam made Cambodia part of the war. To court goodwill with Beijing and Hanoi, Sihanouk broke diplomatic relations with the United States in 1965 during the US escalation of its forces in Indochina. He restored relations with Washington in 1969 and even agreed to US bombing in Cambodia because of his concern that the growth of the PAVN presence in his country was threatening its independence. Other members of the government in Phnom Penh believed that the prince was not doing enough and in March 1970 replaced him as prime minister with the openly pro-American General Lon Nol. Although the US military incursion into Cambodia that followed was brief, the US and DRV extension of the Vietnam War into Cambodia by ground operations and bombing had unleashed a pattern of death, destruction of villages, and dislocation of population that provided fertile political ground for the small Communist Party of Kampuchea (CPK).

The CPK used the traditional name Kampuchea for Cambodia, and its members were often referred to as Khmer Rouge or Red Khmer. By the 1960s, the term Khmer Rouge had come to designate specifically a radical faction within the CPK led by a shadowy figured named Pol Pot, whom many in the party knew only as Brother Number One. Using assassination and terror within the party itself, Pol Pot turned it into an instrument of his extreme notions that Cambodia had nothing to learn from outside influences, including Vietnamese communism as well as Western bourgeois ideologies. His proclaimed vision was a simple agrarian state that rejected modernization and restored the glories of the ancient Angkor kingdom.

After the coup against Sihanouk in 1970 the Khmer Republic, as Lon Nol's government was known, failed to thrive and the Khmer Rouge grew stronger. The republic's army suffered from corruption, poor leadership, and lack of mobility. Massive US bombing of so-called communist 'sanctuaries' in Cambodia failed to prevent Khmer Rouge recruiting and population control in rural areas. In fact, the bombing produced an estimated 2 million refugees and a serious shortage of basic necessities for the general population that collapsed the country's economy. In 1973 the US Congress passed legislation prohibiting further US bombing and, as in the case of South Vietnam, reduced the level of US financial assistance to the inept Phnom Penh government. In January 1975, Khmer Rouge forces laid siege to the capital. On 17 April, after Lon Nol had fled and the US embassy had staged a hasty evacuation of US personnel from the country in a scene to be reenacted days later in Saigon, Phnom Penh fell to the Khmer Rouge.

Pol Pot declared 1975 the 'Year Zero' and set out with his, mostly young, Khmer Rouge soldiers to remake Cambodia into a rural collectivist society. Their program was not a patriotic or social reform of the nation in the mold of the Vietnamese communist program, but was the total eradication of existing society. With the ruthlessness of fanatics, the Khmer Rouge emptied Phnom Penh of essentially its entire population, herded millions of people into forced labor in which many died of starvation or overwork, and executed thousands of teachers, physicians, and other professionals considered to be bourgeois and Westernized. The total of those murdered in what was later labeled 'the killing fields' is estimated to be 1.5 million. It was a genocide of a government against its own people.

The terrible reality of what was occurring in Cambodia was not immediately known to the world, and the initial international perception of the end of the wars in Indochina focused on geopolitical strategy. The People's Republic of China and Democratic Kampuchea, the Khmer Rouge name for Cambodia, formed an alliance. The leaders in both countries claimed to share a common ideology of building agrarian communism, but their principal link was a shared concern about the regional power of a now reunited Vietnam. The historic mistrust between the Chinese and Vietnamese had always strained their wartime partnership, and with the end of the Vietnam War in 1975 Beijing terminated its military aid to the DRV. From Hanoi's perspective, the PRC and Democratic Kampuchea were aligned in a hostile encirclement of Vietnam.

In addition to the threat of regional isolation, the Socialist Republic of Vietnam (SRV), which Hanoi renamed the reunited country in 1976, faced an enormous task of domestic reconstruction from the ravages of war and the legacy of more than a generation of often ruthless internal conflict. Thousands of Vietnamese faced severe economic hardship. The war had left in and near the cities huge numbers of homeless refugees, orphans, amputees, and other physically disabled people, and throughout the country some farmers were without homes, livestock, or implements. The government attempted to address these problems with the creation of economic collectives and other socialist approaches that met resistance from the entrepreneurial South Vietnamese. To punish and discipline their former political and military enemies, the new rulers sent many ARVN officers, RVN officials, teachers, and clergy to reeducation camps. The length of incarceration and conditions in the camps varied, but all required hard labor and imposed harsh punishments for breaking rules. Some detainees were executed. Over a million people spent some time in the camps, and about 50,000 were held for more than five years. Trying to elude imprisonment or acting after release from reeducation, thousands of Vietnamese fled the country, often by boat. Many of these 'boat people' were ethnic Chinese who owned small businesses and faced ethnic and ideological hostility in the SRV. Tens of thousands of them became part of the almost 2 million refugees who left from all parts of Indochina in 1975 and the years immediately following.

As the SRV struggled to rebuild Vietnam and lost the economic assistance of the PRC, it looked for possible help from its former foe the United States. As part of the diplomatic maneuvers to end US military involvement in Vietnam but still keep some negotiating leverage with Hanoi, the Nixon administration had held out the possibility of providing $3.25 billion in post-war reconstruction aid to Vietnam. Congress had specifically prohibited such assistance without a full accounting from Hanoi of American MIAs, but after becoming president in 1977, Jimmy Carter renewed the suggestion that Washington might normalize diplomatic relations with Hanoi if the SRV would cooperate on providing more information about questions of whether some MIAs may have been POWs. With an ever-mounting economic crisis on their hands, Vietnamese officials responded with a firm demand that the United States owed as war reparations the funds that Nixon had offered. No US leader could have taken political responsibility for acquiescing to such demands. Also, Carter was following the path begun by Nixon toward improved US–China relations, and he knew that Beijing would not be happy with US economic assistance for Vietnam. The possibility of an American *rapprochement* with the SRV collapsed. With no US aid forth-coming, Hanoi's leaders, although reluctant to appear dependent, turned to the Soviet Union and signed on 3 November 1978 a formal aid arrangement that allowed Soviet use of former US naval facilities in Vietnam. On 1 January 1979, the United States restored normal relations with Beijing, ending a break of 30 years.

Just days earlier, on 25 December, the PAVN invaded Cambodia and soon ended the Khmer Rouge reign of terror. Leaving a large occupation force in Cambodia, the Vietnamese installed a new Cambodian commu-nist government under Prime Minister Heng Samrin, who had led a party faction opposed to Pol Pot. On 17 February 1979 China sent troops into northern Vietnam in an effort to pressure Hanoi away from what Beijing characterized as an expansionist policy. After only a month, the PRC withdrew its forces and ceased the punitive action, but both China and the United States continued to isolate Vietnam economically and did not publicly acknowledge that Hanoi's actions had been in large part a response to the excesses of the Khmer Rouge. Vietnamese occupation forces left Cambodia in 1989, but it was not until February 1994 that President Bill Clinton finally lifted the US trade embargo against the SRV. On 11 July 1995, Clinton extended formal diplomatic recognition to the government in Hanoi.[13]

US post-war issues

Within the United States, the Vietnam War left behind a number of social, political, and emotional scars. One reason that it took 20 years after the DRV's victory in 1975 before the United States would recog-nize the government in Hanoi was the difficulty that many Americans and their leaders had in accepting US defeat. Emblematic of this prob-lem was the POW/MIA issue. Although Vietnam's occupation of Cambodia was later cited as the reason for delaying the establishment of relations between Washington and Hanoi, the issue of normalization of relations was from the beginning to the end tied to US insistence on a full accounting of the fate of Americans who had been prisoners or who remained missing. Even as the 591 US POWs returned home in 1973, controversy began to swirl around the question of whether or not living American prisoners still remained in Vietnam, Laos, and Cambodia.

Officials in Hanoi reported at the time of the repatriation of prisoners in accordance with the Paris agreement that all who were living had been freed and that 55 had died in captivity. There were more than 2300 men listed officially as MIA, and of this group it was impossible to know how many may have been prisoners at some time. The vast majority of them had died in fiery plane crashes leaving no remains or had become casualties in combat with irregular forces in remote areas throughout Indochina. Neither Vietnamese nor American leaders could ascertain with certainty the final fate of these men and the location of their remains. On many occasions various individuals claimed to have 'evidence' of Americans being seen alive and in captivity. From 1975 into the 1990s, several military and congressional investigations were conducted and none found a single credible case of an American being held prisoner anywhere in Indochina. Most of the so-called live sightings were proven to be intentional hoaxes.

Contrary to evidence and logic, the myth of living US prisoners persisted for years and inhibited the public's ability to reconcile itself to failure of American policy in Indochina. Richard Nixon had first drawn attention to the fate of the POWs as a means of sustaining popular support for his strategy of negotiated withdrawal. The National League of Families of American Prisoners and Missing in Southeast Asia understandably held on to hope that their missing loved ones were alive, and Nixon's encouragement turned the organization into a powerful political lobby. Although the total number of US soldiers and airmen missing in Indochina was small compared to American MIA totals in other wars and was less than one percent of the estimated number of missing Vietnamese, every president from Nixon to Clinton felt politically obligated to stand firm on the need for Hanoi to provide more information on missing Americans. Wanting access to trade and investment desperately needed to rebuild Vietnam, the SRV ultimately went to great lengths to meet this demand and cooperated with US efforts to locate and identify remains. Into the 1990s, however, the United States maintained the economic boycott of its enemy and pressed other nations to follow suit. In 1991, a writer for the *Economist* observed: 'One day Vietnam may overcome the consequences of having won its war against America. The Americans are putting off this day as long as possible.'[14] A prominent part of the 1995 agreement that finally formalized relations between Washington and Hanoi was a pledge from Hanoi of continued participation in joint efforts to locate MIA remains.

Although American culture made a civic religion out of the League of Families' motto 'you are not forgotten,' military veterans who were not missing were, ironically, often ignored by the larger society. Vietnam veterans experienced a general sense of social alienation. Certainly, many reintegrated successfully into domestic life when they came home from the war. In addition, that some veterans would have problems of social readjustment was not unique to this war. In many respects, however, veterans as a group, regardless of their individual circumstances, were initially an embarrassment to many Americans. These were the men, and some women, who had fought a failed and controversial war, and their presence was an uncomfortable reminder of one of the worst public policies in American history. It did not matter that the US decisions to intervene militarily in Vietnam and how to conduct that fight were not of their making. Many citizens did not want to discuss the war and preferred to forget it. Consequently there were no celebrations of the soldiers' heroism and service, no victory parades. The veterans were consciously ignored by some and, incredibly, were blamed by others for what was, in fact, a shared American failure. It was common for veterans to avoid talking about what they had seen and done, except with other veterans who had been there. Some could not hold a job or maintain a personal relationship. These men and women (military nurses in particular) had gone through a physical and emotional ordeal in Vietnam and felt that their fellow Americans not only failed to appreciate them but rejected them.

Some veterans carried heavier burdens than others. A US Veterans Administration (VA) report in 1978 estimated that more than 500,000 Vietnam veterans were physically disabled. Of this group, 9652 were in VA hospitals, where they received free but not always quality care. Some war-related medical problems created particularly tragic situations, such as the effects of exposure to the chemical defoliant Agent Orange. Throughout the war, the US Air Force had conducted aerial spraying of herbicides to remove the dense vegetation that provided cover for enemy ambushes and to deny crop resources to the NLF. Some veterans later developed serious medical conditions, including cancers and birth defects in their children, that laboratory research traced to the chemical dioxin in Agent Orange. For several years the VA disputed veterans' claims that they suffered from war-related dioxin exposure. In 1984 as the result of an out-of-court settlement of a class-action suit against the manufacturers of Agent Orange, afflicted veterans received some compensation for this group of illnesses.[15]

Not all war wounds are physical, and in 1980 the American Psychiatric Association identified a war-related condition called post-traumatic stress disorder (PTSD). Known to soldiers in other wars as 'shell shock' or 'battle fatigue,' PTSD is the diagnosis for severe person-ality changes brought on by the fear and rage experienced by men in combat or the unrelenting emotional stress endured by doctors and nurses constantly treating mangled and dying patients. PTSD afflicted to some degree hundreds of thousands of Vietnam veterans, who exhibited various symptoms, such as agonizing grief, tormenting guilt, suicidal longings, severe depression, sudden acts of violence, or inability to form or maintain close personal relationships. As with Agent Orange, PTSD was not appropriately diagnosed initially. Many medical professionals often looked for other behavioral pathologies and did not realize that the condition was a normal psychological reaction to abnormal stress.[16]

By the middle of the 1980s, the United States was beginning to reconcile itself to the realities of the war. Immediately after the war through much of the 1970s, there was a general avoidance of public discussion, as if the war were a dark family secret about which one did not talk. Occasionally a character in a Hollywood movie might be a Vietnam veteran, but he was usually portrayed as a dangerous misfit. Gradually, however, the popular image of veterans began to change. In some films the action hero was a veteran, and in others, such as *The Deer Hunter*, the veterans were seen more sympathetically as men trying to do their duty. During the years that Ronald Reagan was presi-dent there was a series of movies about rescuing POWs, which both exploited the public attention on that issue and allowed the veteran hero to rescue his comrades. Also shaping public perceptions was a growing body of poetry and fiction written by Vietnam veterans. Much of this literature explored the authors' personal disillusionment and, as a genre, it juxtaposed the destructiveness of the American war in Vietnam against old myths of the nation's moral rectitude. In 1986, Vietnam veteran Oliver Stone directed the film *Platoon*, which was the first of a group of reality films that combined fairly accurate portrayals of combat in Vietnam with an antiwar theme.

The one event as much as any other that helped to mend the social tensions caused by the war was the building of the Vietnam Veterans Memorial in Washington, DC. Dedicated in November 1982, this black granite wall built into a hillside in the heart of the national capital was conceived by Vietnam veterans and largely funded through veterans' contributions. On it are inscribed the names of the more than 58,000 Americans who died in the war or who remain missing. Although some veterans at first thought its modern and simple design did not adequately honor the service and sacrifice of the soldiers, it soon became the most visited site in Washington. Added later were a flagpole, a bronze statue of three combat soldiers, and a bronze statue of three military nurses. The wall and the statues became a place of remembrance and reflection that seemed to open the way for a broader reexamination among Americans of the meaning of the Vietnam experience.

Lessons and legacies

The Vietnam War was a transforming event in late twentieth-century international relations. It extended over 30 years and cost over 2 million Vietnamese lives, 75,000 French deaths, 58,000 American fatalities, and 5000 other deaths (mostly South Korean troops allied with US forces). This major conflict resolved decades of internal political conflict in Vietnam, ended more than a century of direct French and American involvement in the country, and left an independent and united, although problem-plagued, Socialist Republic of Vietnam. These were significant historical milestones for Vietnam and for the entire area of Southeast Asia. Of greatest significance for global security, however, was the impact that the war had on the self-concept and strategic thinking of the United States. In 1945 when the Franco–Vietminh War began, US leaders felt confident about the superiority of American military power and democratic ideals after the American-led Allied victories over the German and Japanese dictatorships. There was fear, to be sure, of the ambitions and potential menace of the Soviet Union, but there was also a sense that the containment policy and its combination of economic, military, and political deterrence would keep America and the world secure. In 1975 when the Vietnam War ended, the mood in America was one of frustration, internal division, and moral uncertainty. Despite the willingness to sacrifice thousands of lives and billions of dollars, the United States had failed to achieve its containment goal of ensuring the survival of a separate and sustainable ally in South Vietnam. The United States had lost the war.

Much of the legacy of this lost war was bitter for Americans. In the triumphant experience of the Second World War, families mourned their losses as noble sacrifices, but for many Americans the deaths of their loved ones in Vietnam seemed to be senseless sacrifices in a futile and perhaps even mistaken cause. Thousands of men who survived returned home with permanent and painful physical disabilities. At a rate four times higher than other wars, veterans suffered severe psychological impairment that one psychiatrist attributed to nagging guilt from the unparalleled extent of the killing of women, children, and the elderly in

US ground and air operations. Another real casualty of the war was the loss of the idealism of Kennedy's and Johnson's reform programs. Much of Johnson's Great Society went unfunded. Instead, deficit spending on the war fueled inflation and added to the cost of living. The decision to fight in Vietnam, the way the war was fought, and the slow process of withdrawal were among the worst public policy decisions in US history. In the process, citizens lost confidence in the ability of government to lead. Public opinion polls in 1976 revealed that only 11 percent of Americans had 'a great deal of confidence' in the executive branch of the US government. In 1966, that number had been 41 percent. Congress suffered a greater decline from 42 percent in 1966 down to 9 percent in 1976. When asked about the military, the public's confidence level fell from 62 percent to 23 percent over the same period.[17]

Defeat prompts recrimination and a search for blame. The most enduring debates have been over the merits of US military intervention in Vietnam and over the way the United States chose to fight the war. There are now dozens of general histories of the war, and most of these argue in some form that US leaders misapplied to Vietnam the containment policy that the Truman administration developed in response to the perceived Soviet threat to Western Europe. Through the 1950s and 1960s, American policy makers assumed that a local victory in Southeast Asia by the Vietnamese communists would be a strategic gain for Moscow and Beijing over US global interests, and they consistently misjudged the depth and resilience of the revolutionary nationalism of Ho Chi Minh and his party. When Washington's economic and military aid failed to build a viable nation in South Vietnam to counter North Vietnam, US air and ground forces intervened directly to defend the RVN and the credibility of America's commitment to international security. Even that Americanization of the war produced only a military stalemate. Belatedly it became clear that the war was not winnable in any meaningful sense. A military victory would require a dramatic increase in the destructive force of the United States against North Vietnam that was not defensible in terms of the peripheral value of the region to US national interests and the human and financial costs of such a course. Finally, according to this liberal–realist critique, Washington began gradually to extricate the United States from a war it should not have undertaken in the first place.[18]

A number of military and civilian officials who participated in these decisions and some historians have disagreed with this negative view and have argued that the war was necessary and winnable. Most of these 'revisionists,' who challenge the prevailing view that the American war was unwarranted and unwinnable, accept the official US rationale that America's purpose was to contain international communist aggression in Southeast Asia and to prevent the imposition of a totalitarian regime on all of Vietnam. There are, however, many differences among the revisionists' interpretations. Some acknowledge that the ability of the United States to provide an external solution to Vietnam's internal conflict was limited, but that justice, ideology, and strategy did not allow the United States the option of doing nothing in response to the armed insurrection against its South Vietnamese allies. Most revisionists, however, both support the decision to intervene and find that there were other more promising roads not taken to victory. A number of military officers who served in Vietnam later wrote that civilian officials in Washington for political reasons artificially restricted the number of troops and level of bombing required to accomplish the mission. This 'stab-in-the-back' scenario was also combined with a belief that conventional military tactics of isolating the battlefield and massing overwhelming force on an objective would have worked better than the unconventional method employed of dispersing forces and chasing after elusive guerrillas. On the other hand, an alternative revisionist school maintains that the US military command in Vietnam did not take the political challenge of the NLF seriously enough. These writers construct a 'win' thesis around better employment of US forces for population security and pacification efforts to give the population reasons to identify with the Saigon government.[19]

It may be more palatable to American analysts to conclude that their nation's problem was that it did not try hard enough or with a correct strategy than to admit that an ignorance of, and arrogance toward, Vietnam lay at the heart of the American debacle. Like the policy makers, these historical interpreters give inadequate attention to the political and social origins of the war and to the corrupt and often repressive nature of the South Vietnamese leadership. There is no question that some communist cadres could be ruthless or that some RVN officials could be public spirited, but the ability of US high-technology warfare or corporate management techniques to mediate an accommodation between the deeply rooted historical differences dividing Hanoi and Saigon was unrealistic. In truth the destructiveness of the American war at the village level served to alienate the people from the RVN government supported by that force. Conversely, when US soldiers built schools and dug wells to win the hearts and minds of villagers, the local political control of an area often reverted right back to the NLF when the Americans moved on to another location. When the PAVN launched its

Ho Chi Minh Campaign in 1975, the military tactics were conventional but a willingness by the ARVN to defend Saigon was not generally apparent. After years of revolutionary warfare, the capital fell, as one historian has put it, like 'an overripe fruit.'[20] The outcome of the war was not just an American failure but was also a North Vietnamese success. The Vietnamese communists combined patriotic appeals with a disciplined political organization to sustain an effective insurgency against the Saigon government that was receiving extensive US assistance. Hanoi's leaders were fallible politicians, and their ultimate victory was not inevitable. They were formidable opponents, however, with a well-conceived revolutionary strategy for resisting and outlasting the powerful Americans.[21]

Understanding how and why the militarily and economically powerful United States failed to gain its objectives in Vietnam is not an idle academic question, but one that remains central to effective US policy making. The United States had made, in effect, a staged retreat from Vietnam, but it remained a mighty nation with far-ranging global interests. In the years immediately after the war, American leaders faced repeated decisions on when, where, and why to engage US power. In Iran, militant Muslim revolutionaries removed from power the American-backed Shah and held American diplomats hostage for over a year. Moscow used this crisis as an opportunity to send its troops into Afghanistan. In Central America, Marxist insurgents forced long-time American client regimes out of office. By the 1980s the term 'Vietnam syndrome' had come into use to denote the reluctance of the public, its representatives in Congress, and even military leaders to support US armed intervention even in such provocative cases. Often expressed as 'no more Vietnams,' the lesson seemed to be a neo-isolationist one that the United States should not put its soldiers and treasure at risk in situations that did not immediately threaten the security of the United States. Former President Nixon and Presidents Ronald Reagan and George H. W. Bush worried, however, that this syndrome prevented the nation from vigorously defending legitimate national interests and from standing up to aggressors. To them 'no more Vietnams' meant that military intervention could be ordered, but only when there was a clearly obtainable goal, explicit political support, and a willingness to use the full extent of American military assets. These guidelines were articulated by Reagan's secretary of defense, Caspar Weinberger, and endorsed by General Colin Powell, who served as Reagan's national security advisor and as chair of the Joint Chiefs of Staff under presidents Bush and Bill Clinton.[22]

In response to Iraq's invasion of Kuwait in August 1990, the admin-

istration of President George H. W. Bush attacked Iraq in 1991. The
military deployment followed the Weinberger-Powell guidelines and a
conventional battle plan of massed forces and rapid movement, another
lesson military planners said derived from the Vietnam experience. After
a preliminary round of high-technology bombing of Baghdad and Iraqi
military installations, the ground phase of the war lasted only 100 hours
and routed the forces of Iraqi leader Saddam Hussein. The president
proclaimed: 'By God, we've kicked the Vietnam syndrome once and for
all.'[23] The weight of the Vietnam precedent remained heavy, however,
because the administration declined to continue the ground war on to
Baghdad itself out of concern that it would become a protracted and
deadly engagement. A similar response occurred later in the 1990s as
President Clinton confronted the terribly brutal ethnic violence that
ripped through the Balkans. When this conflict turned into mass murder
of civilians in the name of 'ethnic cleansing,' the comparisons with the
Nazis' attempted genocide of Jews combined with the strategic
geographic importance of southeastern Europe led the United States and
its NATO allies to wage an air war against Serbia. Worried about the
'quagmire' that Vietnam had been for US ground forces, however,
Clinton publicly declared this action would be limited to air power only.

The influence of the Vietnam War has had an enormous staying
power. The Persian Gulf War of 1991 and the Balkan wars of the 1990s
were a reassertion of American armed might, but did not diminish the
Vietnam-induced constraints policy makers felt on the deployment of
American ground troops. The breakup of the Soviet Union in 1989
removed many of the containment rationales for an interventionist US
foreign policy, but the end of the Cold War did not end the perceived
danger of global threats to peace. Indeed, the long-standing hatred of the
United States by Islamic extremists – who characterized American
cultural and political power as satanic – produced the unprecedented
terrorist attacks on New York and Washington on 11 September 2001.
Soon after, the George W. Bush administration launched US air and
ground attacks in Afghanistan to strike at the al-Qaeda terrorist network
behind the attacks. Arguing that Iraq had ties to the terrorists and that it
possessed weapons of mass destruction that posed possibly imminent
danger to the United States and other nations, the Bush administration
mounted a major war in 2003 that ended the Saddam Hussein regime in
a matter of weeks, but that dragged on as the US occupying forces faced
constant attack from terrorists and guerrillas. Although much smaller
than the Vietnam War – there were 135,000 US troops in Iraq in 2004 –
the Iraq War instantly invited parallels with the earlier conflict. Although

top American officials asserted before the war began that the United States was not engaged in nation building in Iraq as it had attempted in South Vietnam, the difficulty of restoring civil order in Iraq actually revived the phrase 'winning hearts and minds' from the Vietnam pacification efforts. An even more haunting echo of the past was the credibility trap in which the Bush administration found itself, that is, how to begin to reduce the American presence in a much more costly war than it had anticipated without the appearance of abandoning Iraq and the region to further chaos and harm.

The US decision to fight a war in Vietnam, and to continue that war for as long as it did, was shaped primarily by Washington's desire to maintain the credibility of US power and purpose with both friends and foes. The decision only secondarily and vaguely had any roots in the internal historical factors in Vietnam itself. Over time it became obvious that the vast military and economic power of the United States and the democratic ideals about which US leaders liked to boast had only limited applicability in the physical and cultural environment of Vietnam. It was the Vietnamese, not the Americans, who were the principal actors in their own drama. If there is one general historical lesson to be drawn from the American experience in Vietnam, it is that local history and culture set real limits on the effectiveness of external force, no matter how great that force may be. The United States had one failed war in Vietnam, and for a great and wise nation, one Vietnam War should be enough.

Notes

1 Causes: Colonialism and containment

1. Joseph Buttinger, *A Dragon Defiant: A Short History of Vietnam* (New York: Praeger, 1971), pp. 7–12.
2. Keith Weller Taylor, *The Birth of Vietnam* (Berkeley: University of California Press, 1983), p. 28.
3. Ibid., pp. 130, 299–301; John T. McAlister Jr., *Viet Nam: The Origins of Revolution* (New York: Knopf, 1969), pp. 30–5.
4. Joseph Buttinger, *Vietnam: A Political History* (New York: Praeger, 1972), pp. 13, 51–2.
5. McAlister, *Viet Nam*, pp. 36–7.
6. Buttinger, *A Dragon Defiant*, pp. 53–7.
7. McAlister, *Viet Nam*, pp. 39–51.
8. David G. Marr, *Vietnamese Anticolonialism* (Berkeley: University of California Press, 1971), pp. 196–7.
9. Buttinger, *Vietnam*, pp. 146–7.
10. David G. Marr, *Vietnamese Tradition on Trial, 1920–1945* (Berkeley: University of California Press, 1981), pp. 373–6.
11. The authoritative English-language biography of Ho is William J. Duiker, *Ho Chi Minh* (New York: Hyperion, 2000).
12. Ibid., 251–4.
13. Mark Philip Bradley, *Imagining Vietnam and America: The Making of Postcolonial Vietnam, 1919–1950* (Chapel Hill: University of North Carolina Press, 2000), pp. 134–40.
14. William J. Duiker, *Sacred War: Nationalism and Revolution in a Divided Vietnam* (New York: McGraw-Hill, 1995), p. 48.
15. Ibid., p. 49.
16. Gareth Porter, ed., *Vietnam: A History in Documents* (New York: New American Library, 1981), p. 43.
17. Spencer C. Tucker, *Vietnam* (Lexington: University Press of Kentucky, 1999), pp. 53–6.

18. Duiker, *Sacred War*, 62–4.
19. Ellen Hammer, *The Struggle for Indochina, 1940–1955* (Stanford, CA: Stanford University Press, 1966), pp. 233–43.
20. Bradley, *Imagining Vietnam and America*, p. 178.
21. *Public Papers of the Presidents of the United States: Harry S. Truman, 1947* (Washington, DC: Government Printing Office, 1963), pp. 176–80.
22. Gary R. Hess, *The United States' Emergence as a Southeast Asian Power, 1940–1950* (New York: Columbia University Press, 1987), pp. 333–71; Lloyd C. Gardner, *Approaching Vietnam: From World War II through Dienbienphu* (New York: Norton, 1988), pp. 80–92.
23. George McT. Kahin, *Intervention: How America Became Involved in Vietnam* (New York: Knopf, 1986), pp. 36–7, 42; Ronald H. Spector, *Advice and Support: The Early Years, 1941–1960* (Washington, DC: Government Printing Office, 1983), pp. 119–65.

2   Commitments: Dwight D. Eisenhower, John F. Kennedy, and Ngo Dinh Diem

1. *Public Papers of the Presidents of the United States: Dwight Eisenhower, 1953* (Washington, DC: Government Printing Office, 1958), p. 16.
2. Dwight D. Eisenhower, *Crusade in Europe* (Garden City, NY: Doubleday, 1948), p. 476.
3. *Public Papers of the Presidents of the United States: Dwight Eisenhower, 1960* (Washington, DC: Government Printing Office, 1961), pp. 1035–40. See also Clark Clifford memorandum to Lyndon Johnson, 29 September 1967, United States Department of Defense, *The Pentagon Papers: The Defense Department History of United States Decision Making on Vietnam*, Senator Gravel edition, 4 vols (Boston, MA: Beacon Press, 1971), 2:635–7.
4. John L. Gaddis, *Strategies of Containment: A Critical Appraisal of Postwar American National Security Policy* (New York: Oxford University Press, 1982), pp. 145–61.
5. United States Senate, *Executive Sessions of the Senate Foreign Relations Committee* (Historical Series), vol. 5, 83d Cong., 1st sess., 1953 (Washington, DC: Government Printing Office, 1977), pp. 385–8.
6. George McT. Kahin, *Intervention: How America Became Involved in Vietnam* (New York: Knopf, 1986), p. 42; George C. Herring, *America's Longest War: The United States and Vietnam, 1950–1975*, 4th edn (New York: McGraw-Hill, 2002), pp. 30–6.
7. Arthur W. Radford, *From Pearl Harbor to Vietnam: The Memoirs of Admiral Arthur W. Radford*, ed. Stephen Jurika Jr. (Stanford, CA: Hoover Institution Press, 1980), pp. 391–5; Ronald H. Spector, *Advice and Support: The Early Years, 1941–1960* (Washington, DC: Government Printing

Office, 1983), pp. 199–202; John Prados, *The Sky Would Fall: Operation Vulture: The Secret U.S. Bombing Mission to Vietnam, 1954* (New York: Dial Press, 1983), pp. 152–6.

8. *Department of State Bulletin*, 12 April 1954, pp. 539–42.

9. *Public Papers of the Presidents of the United States: Dwight Eisenhower, 1954* (Washington, DC: Government Printing Office, 1958), pp. 332–3.

10. Arthur Minnich memorandum of conversation, no date, United States Department of State, *Foreign Relations of the United States, 1952–1954*, vol. 13, *Indochina* (Washington, DC: Government Printing Office, 1982), p. 1413. (*Foreign Relations of the United States* will hereafter be cited as *FRUS*.)

11. Melanie Billings-Yun, *Decision Against War: Eisenhower and Dien Bien Phu, 1954* (New York: Columbia University Press, 1988); Richard E. Neustadt, *Presidential Power and the Modern Presidents: The Politics of Leadership from Roosevelt to Reagan* (New York: Free Press, 1990), pp. 295–302; Richard H. Immerman, 'Between the Unattainable and the Unacceptable: Eisenhower and Dienbienphu,' in Richard A. Melanson and David Myers, eds, *Reevaluating Eisenhower: American Foreign Policy in the Fifties* (Urbana: University of Illinois Press, 1987), pp. 120–1, 142–4.

12. George C. Herring and Richard H. Immerman, 'Eisenhower, Dulles, and Dienbienphu: "The Day We Didn't Go to War" Revisited,' *Journal of American History* 71 (September 1984): 343–63; and Robert J. McMahon, 'Eisenhower and Third World Nationalism: A Critique of the Revisionists,' *Political Science Quarterly* 101 (Fall 1986): 453–73.

13. *FRUS, 1952–54*, vol. 16, *The Geneva Conference* (Washington, DC: Government Printing Office, 1981), pp. 1505–42. Herring, *America's Longest War*, pp. 45–9; Lloyd C. Gardner, *Approaching Vietnam: From World War II through Dienbienphu, 1941–1954* (New York: Norton, 1988), pp, 248–56, 281–4.

14. *FRUS, 1952–54*, 13:1870.

15. Memorandum of conversation, 29 June 1954, *FRUS, 1952–54*, vol. 12, *East Asia and the Pacific* (Washington, DC: Government Printing Office, 1984), p. 588; *Department of State Bulletin* (20 September 1954): 394–6.

16. John P. Burke and Fred I. Greenstein, *How Presidents Test Reality: Decisions on Vietnam, 1954 and 1965* (New York: Russell Sage Foundation, 1989), pp. 269–70; David L. Anderson, 'China Policy and Presidential Politics, 1952,' *Presidential Studies Quarterly* 10 (Winter 1980): 79–90.

17. Eisenhower to Alfred M. Gruenther, 8 June 1954, FRUS, 1952–54, 13:1667–69.

18. Discussion at the 218th NSC meeting, 22 October, 1954, ibid., 2157.

19. David L. Anderson, *Trapped by Success: The Eisenhower Administration and Vietnam, 1953–1961* (New York: Columbia University Press, 1991), pp. 52–5.

20. Collins to Dulles, 31 March 1955, and 7 April 1955, *FRUS, 1955–57*, vol.

1, *Vietnam* (Washington, DC: Government Printing Office, 1985), pp. 168–71, 218–21; Dulles to Collins, 20 April 1955, ibid., pp. 270–2 (Dulles's italics). See also Eisenhower to Collins, 3 November 1954, *FRUS, 1952–54*, 13:2207.

21. *FRUS, 1955–57*, 1:294–6.
22. J. Lawton Collins, *Lightning Joe: An Autobiography* (Baton Rouge: Louisiana State University Press, 1979), pp. 405–7.
23. John Foster Dulles, 'An Historic Week – Report to the President,' 17 May 1955, pp. 4–5, box 91, John Foster Dulles Papers, Princeton University Library.
24. For a good description of Diem's Vietnam see Robert Scigliano, *South Vietnam: Nation under Stress* (Boston, MA: Houghton Mifflin, 1963).
25. William J. Sebald memorandum to Dulles, 10 May 1956, *FRUS, 1955–57*, 1:680–2; Kahin, Intervention, pp. 88–92.
26. Kenneth T. Young memorandum to Walter S. Robertson, 5 October 1955, Young to G. Frederick Reinhardt, 5 October 1955, *FRUS, 1955–57*, 1:550–4.
27. Reinhardt to Dept of State, 29 November 1955, ibid., 589–92; Reinhardt to Dulles, 3 March 1956, file 751G.00/3–356, and Reinhardt to Dulles, 8 March 1956, file 751G.00/3–856, United States Department of State General Records, Record Group 59, National Archives, Washington, DC (hereafter cited as RG 59).
28. Reinhardt to Dulles, 6 December 1955, file 751G.00/12–655, RG 59; G. Frederick Reinhardt interview by Philip A. Crowl, 30 October 1965, John Foster Dulles Oral History Project, Princeton University Library; Bernard B. Fall, *The Two Viet-Nams: A Political and Military Analysis*, rev. edn (New York: Praeger, 1964), 246–68.
29. Arthur Z. Gardiner to Dept of State, 2 August 1956, file 751G.5–MSP/8–256, and C. E. Lilien memorandum of conversation, 10 December 1957, file 751G.131/12–1057, RG 59; Kahin, *Intervention*, pp. 84–8.
30. Scigliano, *South Vietnam*, p. 193; Fall, *Two Viet-Nams*, pp. 289–306.
31. Program for Ngo Dinh Diem Visit, 3 May 1957, box 73, Subject series, White House Central Files (Confidential File), Eisenhower Library; Burton I. Kaufman, *Trade and Aid: Eisenhower's Foreign Economic Policy* (Baltimore, MD: Johns Hopkins University Press, 1982), pp. 99–110.
32. *Department of State Bulletin* (27 May 1957): 851; *Public Papers of the Presidents of the United States: Dwight Eisenhower, 1957* (Washington, DC: Government Printing Office, 1958), p. 417.
33. Elbridge Durbrow memorandum of conversation, 9 May 1957, *FRUS, 1955–57*, 1:794–9.
34. Joseph G. Morgan, *The Vietnam Lobby: The American Friends of Vietnam, 1955–1975* (Chapel Hill, University of North Carolina Press, 1997), p. 41. William C. Gibbons, *The U.S. Government and the Vietnam War: Executive*

and Legislative Roles and Relationships, part 1, 1945–1960 (Princeton, NJ: Princeton University Press, 1986), pp. 301–5, 320–7.

35. Kahin, *Intervention*, pp, 109–15; Jeffrey Race, *War Comes to Long An: Revolutionary Conflict in a Vietnamese Province* (Berkeley: University of California Press, 1972), pp. 105–22; William J. Duiker, *The Communist Road to Power in Vietnam* (Boulder, CO: Westview Press, 1981), pp. 187–99. Dulles to Durbrow, 19 November 1957, *FRUS, 1955–57*, 1:863–4.

36. Durbrow to Christian Herter, 3 May 1960, Durbrow to Daniel V. Anderson, 18 July 1960, *FRUS, 1958–60*, vol. 1, *Vietnam* (Washington, DC: Government Printing Office, 1986), pp. 433–7, 514-15.

37. Lansdale to Edward J. O'Donnell, 20 September 1960, ibid., p. 580. See also memorandum prepared in Dept of Defense, 4 May 1960, ibid., pp. 439-41; and Samuel T. Williams to R. E. Lawless, 15 May 1962, box 8, Samuel T. Williams Papers, Hoover Institution Archives, Stanford, California.

38. Durbrow to Richard E. Usher, 18 April 1960, *FRUS, 1958–60*, 1:394.

39. Military History Institute of Vietnam, *Victory in Vietnam: The Official History of the People's Army of Vietnam, 1954–1975*, trans. Merle L. Pribbenow (Lawrence: University Press of Kansas, 2002), p. 50.

40. Anderson, *Trapped by Success*, p. 195.

41. *Public Papers of the Presidents of the United States: John F. Kennedy, 1961* (Washington, DC: Government Printing Office, 1962), p. 1.

42. Gary R. Hess, 'Commitment in the Age of Counterinsurgency: Kennedy's Vietnam Options and Decisions, 1961–1963,' in David L. Anderson, ed., *Shadow on the White House: Presidents and the Vietnam War, 1945–1975* (Lawrence: University Press of Kansas, 1993), p. 69.

43. National Security Action Memorandum No. 52, 11 May 1961, *FRUS, 1961–1963*, vol. 1, *Vietnam, 1961* (Washington, DC: Government Printing Office, 1988), p. 133. See also 'A Program of Action to Prevent Communist Domination of South Vietnam,' 1 May 1961, ibid., pp. 93–115.

44. William J. Duiker, *Sacred War: Nationalism and Revolution in a Divided Vietnam* (New York: McGraw-Hill, 1995), pp. 139–50.

45. Maxwell Taylor to Kennedy, 3 November 1961, *FRUS, 1961–63*, 1:479–503; National Security Action Memorandum No. 111, 22 November 1961, ibid., pp. 656–7; Chester Bowles, *Promises to Keep: My Years in Public life, 1949–1969* (New York: Harper & Row, 1971), pp. 408–9.

46. Statistics on US military personnel in South Vietnam are from US Department of Defense, OASD (Comptroller), Directorate for Information, Washington, DC.

47. Gary R. Hess, *Vietnam and the United States: Origins and Legacy of War* (Boston, MA: Twayne, 1990), pp. 73–5; Neil Sheehan, *A Bright Shining Lie: John Paul Vann and America in Vietnam* (New York: Random House, 1988), pp. 203–65.

48. Kahin, *Intervention*, pp. 146–82; Ellen J. Hammer, *A Death in November:*

America in Vietnam, 1963 (New York: Oxford University Press, 1987), pp. 177–310.

49. Fredrik Logevall, *Choosing War: The Lost Chance for Peace and the Escalation of War in Vietnam* (Berkeley: University of California Press, 1999), pp. 396–400; Lawrence Freedman, *Kennedy's Wars: Berlin, Cuba, Laos, and Vietnam* (New York: Oxford University Press, 2000), pp. 400–13; David Kaiser, *American Tragedy: Kennedy, Johnson, and the Origins of the Vietnam War* (Cambridge, MA: Harvard University Press, 2000), pp. 3–5, 265; Howard Jones, *Death of a Generation: How the Assassinations of Diem and JFK Prolonged the Vietnam War* (New York: Oxford University Press, 2003), pp. 452–6.

50. *Public Papers of the Presidents of the United States: John F. Kennedy, 1963* (Washington, DC: Government Printing Office, 1964), p. 660.

51. Hess, 'Commitment in the Age of Counterinsurgency,' pp. 81–3; Hammer, *A Death in November*, p. 211; Jeffrey J. Clarke, *Advice and Support: The Final Years* (Washington, DC: Government Printing Office, 1988), p. 275.

3   Credibility: Lyndon Johnson's war

1. Telephone Conversation between Johnson and McGeorge Bundy, 31 May 1965, 12:45 p.m., Citation #7852, Recordings and Transcripts of Telephone Conversations, Lyndon Baines Johnson Library, Austin, Texas (hereafter cited as LBJ Library).

2. Quoted in George C. Herring, 'The Reluctant Warrior: Lyndon Johnson as Commander in Chief,' in David L. Anderson, ed., *Shadow on the White House: Presidents and the Vietnam War, 1945–1975* (Lawrence: University Press of Kansas, 1993), p. 96.

3. A. J. Langguth, *Our Vietnam: The War, 1954–1975* (New York: Simon & Schuster, 2000), p. 269.

4. National Security Action Memorandum No. 273, 26 November 1963, *Foreign Relations of the United States, 1961–63*, vol. 4, *Vietnam, August–December 1963* (Washington, DC: Government Printing Office, 1991), pp. 637–40.

5. Quoted in George C. Herring, *America's Longest War: The United States in Vietnam, 1950–1975*, 4th edn (Boston, MA: McGraw-Hill, 2002), p. 132.

6. Doris Kearns, *Lyndon Johnson and the American Dream* (New York: New American Library, 1976), p. 264.

7. On Johnson's leadership style see George C. Herring, *LBJ and Vietnam: A Different Kind of War* (Austin: University of Texas Press, 1994); and Lloyd C. Gardner, *Pay Any Price: Lyndon Johnson and the Wars for Vietnam* (Chicago: Ivan R. Dee, 1995).

8. Herring, *America's Longest War*, pp. 138–41.

9. Quoted in Robert S. McNamara with Brian VanDeMark, *In Retrospect:*

The Tragedy and Lessons of Vietnam (New York: Times Books, 1995), p. 134.

10. Edwin E. Moïse, *Tonkin Gulf and the Escalation of the Vietnam War* (Chapel Hill: University of North Carolina Press, 1996), pp. 210–11.
11. *Department of State Bulletin* (24 August 1964), 268.
12. Brian VanDeMark, *Into the Quagmire: Lyndon Johnson and the Escalation of the Vietnam War* (New York: Oxford University Press, 1991), pp. 23–6; William J. Duiker, *Sacred War: Nationalism and Revolution in a Divided Vietnam* (New York: McGraw-Hill, 1995), pp. 166–72; Fredrik Logevall, *Choosing War: The Lost Chance for Peace and the Escalation of War in Vietnam* (Berkeley: University of California Press, 1999), pp. 270–3.
13. McGeorge Bundy to Johnson, 7 February 1965, *FRUS, 1964–1968*, vol. 2, *Vietnam, January–June 1965* (Washington, DC: Government Printing Office, 1996), pp. 174–85; Lyndon Baines Johnson, *Vantage Point: Perspectives of the Presidency, 1963–1969* (New York: Popular Library, 1971), pp. 121–32; Herring, *America's Longest War*, 173.
14. Quoted in ibid., p. 162.
15. Bui Diem with David Chanoff, *In the Jaws of History* (Boston, MA: Houghton Mifflin, 1987), p. 127.
16. Quoted in Herring, *America's Longest War*, p. 163.
17. Robert McNamara to Johnson, 1 July 1965, *FRUS, 1964–1968*, vol. 3, *Vietnam, June–December 1965* (Washington, DC: Government Printing Office, 1996), pp. 97–104.
18. Notes of meeting, 20 March, 1968, Tom Johnson's Meeting Notes, box 2, LBJ Library.
19. Lady Bird Johnson, *A White House Diary* (New York: Holt, Rinehart and Winston, 1970), p. 248.
20. Johnson, *Vantage Point*, p. 136.
21. *Public Papers of the Presidents of the United States: Lyndon B. Johnson, 1965* (Washington, DC: Government Printing Office, 1968), 2:794–6.
22. Herring, *America's Longest War*, pp, 161–7; Larry Berman, *Planning a Tragedy* (New York: W. W. Norton, 1982), pp. 105–53.
23. *Public Papers of the Presidents of the United States: Lyndon B. Johnson, 1965* (Washington, DC: Government Printing Office, 1967), 1:394–9.
24. Stanley Karnow, *Vietnam: A History* (New York: Penguin Books, 1984), p. 419; Johnson, *Vantage Point*, p. 134.
25. Herring, *America's Longest War*, p. 160.
26. Intelligence Memorandum, 15 April 1965, FRUS, 1964–68, 2:558–60; Allen E. Goodman, *The Lost Peace: America's Search for a Negotiated Settlement of the Vietnam War* (Stanford, CA: Hoover Institution Press, 1978), pp. 23–8.
27. William C. Westmoreland, *A Soldier Reports* (New York: Dell, 1976), pp. 198–9.

28. George Donelson Moss, *Vietnam: An American Ordeal*, 4th edn (Upper Saddle River, NJ: Prentice Hall, 2002), pp. 215–18.
29. Andrew Goodpaster memorandum, 3 August 1965, Palm Desert-Indio series, box 9, Dwight D. Eisenhower Library, Abilene, Kansas.
30. Telephone Conversation between Johnson and Robert McNamara, 22 December 1965, 10:10 a.m., Citation #9327, Recordings and Transcripts of Telephone Conversations, LBJ Library.
31. Telephone Conversation between Johnson and Maxwell Taylor, 27 December 1965, 8:56 p.m., Citation #9339, ibid.
32. Herring, *America's Longest War*, pp, 167, 186–8.
33. Ibid., pp. 203–4.
34. Gary R. Hess, *Presidential Decisions for War: Korea, Vietnam, and the Persian Gulf* (Baltimore, MD: Johns Hopkins University Press, 2001), pp. 126–8.
35. Hess, *Vietnam*, pp. 97–8; Moss, *Vietnam*, pp. 222–7.
36. Jonathan Schell, *The Real War: The Classic Reporting on the Vietnam War* (New York: Pantheon Books, 1987), p. 188.
37. Ilya V. Gaiduk, 'Developing an Alliance: The Soviet Union and Vietnam, 1954–75,' in Peter Lowe, ed., *The Vietnam War* (Basingstoke: Macmillan – now Palgrave Macmillan, 1998), pp. 143–5.
38. Chen Jian, *Mao's China and the Cold War* (Chapel Hill: University of North Carolina Press, 2001), p. 214.
39. Ibid., pp. 215–29.
40. Walt Rostow, notes of meeting, 17 February 1967, *FRUS, 1964–1968*, vol. 5, *Vietnam 1967* (Washington, DC: Government Printing Office, 2002), p. 185.
41. Hess, *Presidential Decisions for War*, p. 129.
42. McNamara to Johnson, 19 May 1967, *FRUS, 1964–1968*, 5:437.
43. McNamara, *In Retrospect*, p. 307.
44. McNamara to Johnson, 1 November 1967, *FRUS, 1964–1968*, 5:949–50.
45. Jim Jones to Johnson, 2 November 1967, ibid., pp. 954–70.
46. McNamara, *In Retrospect*, p. 309.
47. George W. Allen, *None So Blind: A Personal Account of the Intelligence Failure in Vietnam* (Chicago: Ivan R. Dee, 2001), pp. 237–42.
48. Karnow, *Vietnam*, p. 514.
49. Ibid., pp. 491–8; Hess, *Vietnam*, pp. 99–102.
50. Johnson memorandum, 18 December 1967, *FRUS, 1964–1968*, 5:1118–20.

4 Contention: Antiwar protests, the Tet offensive, and a tumultuous election

1. Melvin Small, *Antiwarriors: The Vietnam War and the Battle for America's Hearts and Minds* (Wilmington, DE: Scholarly Resources, 2002), pp. 22, 34–6.

2. Charles DeBenedetti with Charles Chatfield, *An American Ordeal: The Antiwar Movement of the Vietnam Era* (Syracuse, NY: Syracuse University Press, 1990), pp. 145, 162; Robert Mann, *A Grand Delusion: America's Descent into Vietnam* (New York: Basic Books, 2001), pp. 487–95.
3. Small, *Antiwarriors*, pp. 75–83.
4. Tom Wells, 'The Anti-Vietnam War Movement in the United States,' in Peter Lowe, ed., *The Vietnam War* (Basingstoke: Macmillan – now Palgrave Macmillan, 1998), 121–2.
5. Military History Institute of Vietnam, *Victory in Vietnam: The Official History of the People's Army of Vietnam, 1954–1975*, trans. Merle L. Pribbenow (Lawrence: University Press of Kansas, 2002), pp. 206–23.
6. William S. Turley, *The Second Indochina War: A Short Political and Military History, 1954–1975* (Boulder, CO: Westview Press, 1986), pp. 99–117; George C. Herring, *America's Longest War: The United States and Vietnam, 1950–1975*, 4th edn (Boston: McGraw-Hill, 2002), pp. 225–34.
7. Robert Buzzanco, *Masters of War: Military Dissent and Politics in the Vietnam Era* (Cambridge: Cambridge University Press, 1996), pp. 311–40 (quote on p. 311).
8. Notes of meeting, 'March 26, 1968, 10:30 AM, Meeting with Gen. Wheeler, JCS, and Gen. Creighton Abrams,' Tom Johnson's Notes of Meetings, box 2, Lyndon Baines Johnson Library, Austin, Texas.
9. Notes of Meeting, 26 March 1968, *Foreign Relations of the United States, 1964–1968*, vol. 6, *Vietnam January–August 1968* (Washington, DC: Government Printing Office, 2002), pp. 471–4.
10. Clark Clifford with Richard Holbrooke, *Counsel to the President: A Memoir* (New York: Anchor Books, 1991), p. 518.
11. *Department of State Bulletin*, 15 April 1968, pp. 481–6.
12. Doris Kearns, *Lyndon Johnson and the American Dream* (New York: New American Library, 1976), p. 360.
13. Ronald H. Spector, *After Tet: The Bloodiest Year of the War* (New York: Free Press, 1993), pp. 24–5; Military History Institute, *Victory in Vietnam*, pp. 228–30; Shelby L. Stanton, *The Rise and Fall of an American Army: U.S. Ground Forces in Vietnam, 1965–1973* (San Rafael, CA: Presidio Press, 1985), pp. 259–60.
14. David L. Anderson, ed., *Facing My Lai: Moving Beyond the Massacre* (Lawrence: University Press of Kansas, 1998), pp. 1–16; Michael D. Sallah and Mitch Weiss, 'Buried Secrets, Brutal Truth,' *Toledo (Ohio) Blade*, 22 October 2003.
15. Herring, *America's Longest War*, pp. 257–9.
16. Summary Notes of the 568th Meeting of the National Security Council, 22 May 1968, *FRUS, 1964–1968*, 6:702. Herring, *Longest War*, pp. 252–7.
17. David Broder, 'Election of 1968,' in Arthur M. Schlesinger Jr. and Fred L. Israel, eds, *History of American Presidential Elections, 1789–1968*, 4 vols (New York: Chelsea House, 1971), p. 3718; Philip E. Converse et al.,

'Continuity and Change in American Politics: Parties and Issues in the 1968 Election,' *American Political Science Review* 63 (December 1969): 1092.

18. James R. Jones, 'Behind LBJ's Decision Not to Run in '68,' *New York Times*, 16 April 1988, p. 31.

19. Joseph A. Palermo, *In His Own Right: The Political Odyssey of Senator Robert F. Kennedy* (New York: Columbia University Press, 2001), p. 180.

20. David Farber and Beth Bailey, *The Columbia Guide to America in the 1960s* (New York: Columbia University Press, 2001), p. 189.

21. Richard M. Nixon, 'Asia after Vietnam,' *Foreign Affairs* 46 (October 1967): 111; Jeffrey P. Kimball, '"Peace with Honor": Richard Nixon and the Diplomacy of Threat and Symbolism,' in Anderson, *Shadow on the White House*, pp. 152–3.

22. Hubert H. Humphrey, *The Education of a Public Man* (Garden City, NY: Doubleday, 1976), p. 403.

23. Lyndon Johnson, *The Vantage Point: Perspectives of the Presidency, 1963–1969* (New York: Popular Library, 1971), pp. 513–29.

24. Robert D. Schulzinger, *A Time for War: The United States and Vietnam, 1941–1975* (New York: Oxford University Press, 1997), pp. 271–2.

5   Consequences: Richard Nixon's war

1. Jeffrey P. Kimball, '"Peace with Honor": Richard Nixon and the Diplomacy of Threat and Symbolism,' in David L. Anderson, ed., *Shadow on the White House* (Lawrence: University Press of Kansas, 1993), p. 154.

2. C. L. Sulzberger, *Seven Continents and Forty Years* (New York: Quadrangle, 1977), pp. 505–7.

3. Henry Kissinger, 'The Vietnam Negotiations,' *Foreign Affairs* 47 (January 1969): 234.

4. H. R. Haldeman with Joseph DiMona, *The Ends of Power* (New York: Times Books, 1978), p. 81. On Nixon's 'plan' see Jeffrey Kimball, *Nixon's Vietnam War* (Lawrence: University Press of Kansas, 1998), pp. 97–100.

5. David Broder, 'Election of 1968,' in Arthur M. Schlesinger Jr. and Fred L. Israel, eds, *History of American Presidential Elections, 1789–1968*, 4 vols (New York: Chelsea House, 1971), p. 3747.

6. Earl H. Tilford Jr., 'Operation ROLLING THUNDER,' in Spencer C. Tucker, ed., *Encyclopedia of the Vietnam War: A Political, Social, and Military History*, 3 vols (Santa Barbara, CA: ABC-Clio, 1998), 2:617–20.

7. Henry Kissinger, *The White House Years* (Boston, MA: Little, Brown, 1979), pp. 255–6.

8. Haldeman, *Ends of Power*, pp. 82–3.

9. Jeffrey P. Kimball, *The Vietnam War Files: Uncovering the Secret History of Nixon-Era Strategy* (Lawrence: University Press of Kansas, 2004), pp. 15–19; Kimball, *Nixon's Vietnam War*, pp. 76–86.

10. Quoted in Eric M. Bergerud, *The Dynamics of Defeat: The Vietnam War in Hau Nghia Province* (Boulder, CO: Westview Press, 1991), p. 234; George D. Moss, *Vietnam: An American Ordeal*, 4th edn (Upper Saddle River, NJ: Prentice Hall, 2002), pp. 327–8.
11. Kimball, ' "Peace with Honor," ' p. 162.
12. Melvin Small, 'Containing Domestic Enemies: Richard M. Nixon and the War at Home,' in Anderson, *Shadow on the White House*, pp. 138–40.
13. *Public Papers of the Presidents of the United States: Richard Nixon, 1969* (Washington, DC: Government Printing Office, 1971), 901–9.
14. Kimball, *Vietnam War Files*, pp. 25, 106–7.
15. Jeffrey J. Clark, *Advice and Support: The Final Years* (Washington, DC: Government Printing Office, 1988), pp. 275, 358–9.
16. Moss, *Vietnam*: pp. 349–57.
17. Guenter Lewy, *America in Vietnam* (New York: Oxford University Press, 1978), pp. 406–7.
18. *Public Papers of the Presidents of the United States: Richard Nixon, 1970* (Washington, DC: Government Printing Office, 1971), pp. 405–10.
19. Seymour Hersh, *The Price of Power: Kissinger in the Nixon White House* (New York: Summit, 1983), p. 191.
20. Richard M. Nixon, *RN: The Memoirs of Richard Nixon* (New York: Warner Books, 1978), p. 457; Kissinger, *White House Years*, pp. 511–12; William Shawcross, *Sideshow: Kissinger, Nixon and the Destruction of Cambodia* (New York: Simon & Schuster, 1979), pp. 146–54.
21. Melvin Small, *Antiwarriors: The Vietnam War and the Battle for America's Hearts and Minds* (Wilmington, DE: Scholarly Resources, 2002), pp. 123–33.
22. Kimball, *Vietnam War Files*, pp. 27, 134–8.
23. Ibid., p. 187.
24. Lewy, *America in Vietnam*, p. 407.
25. Gary R. Hess, *Vietnam and the United States: Origins and Legacy of War* (Boston, MA: Twayne, 1990), pp. 124–7.
26. Marvin E. Gettleman et al., eds, *Vietnam and America: A Documented History*, 2nd edn (New York: Grove Press, 1995), pp. 456–9.
27. David L. Anderson, ed., *Facing My Lai: Moving Beyond the Massacre* (Lawrence: University Press of Kansas, 1998), p. 1.
28. George C. Herring, *America's Longest War: The United States and Vietnam, 1950–1975*, 4th edn (Boston, MA: McGraw-Hill, 2002), pp. 298–300.
29. Kissinger, *White House Years*, p. 1018; Pierre Asselin, *A Bitter Peace: Washington, Hanoi, and the Making of the Paris Agreement* (Chapel Hill: University of North Carolina Press, 2002), pp. 27–8.
30. Kimball, *Vietnam War Files*, pp. 29–30, 198; Kissinger, *White House Years*, 1021–31.
31. Marilyn B. Young, *The Vietnam Wars, 1945–1990* (New York: HarperCollins, 1991), pp. 264–5.

32. Qiang Zhai, *China and the Vietnam Wars, 1950–1975* (Chapel Hill: University of North Carolina Press, 2000), pp. 200–1; Ilya V. Gaiduk, *The Soviet Union and the Vietnam War* (Chicago: Ivan R. Dee, 1996), pp. 239–40.
33. Kimball, *Nixon's Vietnam War*, pp. 338–48.
34. Larry Berman, *No Peace, No Honor: Nixon, Kissinger, and Betrayal in Vietnam* (New York: The Free Press, 2001), pp. 82–102.
35. Kimball, *Vietnam War Files*, p. 263.
36. Ibid., p. 274.
37. Nixon to Thieu, 5 January 1973, in Nguyen Tien Hung and Jerrold L. Schecter, *The Palace File* (New York: Harper & Row, 1986), p. 392; Kimball, "'Peace with Honor,'" 174–6; Hess, *Vietnam*, 132–5.
38. *United States Treaties and Other International Agreements*, vol. 24, part 1, 1973 (Washington, DC: Government Printing Office, 1974), pp. 1–225.

6   Conclusions: Peace at last and lasting legacies

1. Arnold R. Isaacs, *Without Honor: Defeat in Vietnam and Cambodia* (New York: Vintage Books, 1984), pp. 69–70, 447–77.
2. David L. Anderson, *The Columbia Guide to the Vietnam War* (New York: Columbia University Press, 2002), p. 286; Lewis Sorley, *A Better War: The Unexamined Victories and Final Tragedy of America's Last Years in Vietnam* (New York: Harcourt Brace, 1999), pp. 361–2.
3. Gary R. Hess, *Vietnam and the United States: Origins and Legacy of War* (Boston, MA: Twayne, 1990), pp. 135–7; Sorley, *A Better War*, pp. 363–4.
4. George C. Herring, *America's Longest War: The United States and Vietnam, 1950–1975*, 4th edn (Boston, MA: McGraw-Hill, 2002), p. 327; Guenter Lewy, *America in Vietnam* (New York: Oxford University Press, 1978), pp. 206–7; Anderson, *Columbia Guide to the Vietnam War*, pp. 173–4.
5. Larry Berman, *No Peace, No Honor: Nixon, Kissinger, and Betrayal in Vietnam* (New York: The Free Press, 2001), pp. 7–9, 204; Jeffrey Kimball, *The Vietnam War Files: Uncovering the Secret History of Nixon-Era Strategy* (Lawrence: University Press of Kansas, 2004), pp. 32–41.
6. For a concise history of the Watergate scandal see Keith W. Olson, *Watergate: The Presidential Scandal that Shook America* (Lawrence: University Press of Kansas, 2003).
7. David L. Anderson, 'Gerald R. Ford and the Presidents' War in Vietnam,' in David L. Anderson, ed., *Shadow on the White House* (Lawrence: University Press of Kansas, 1993), pp. 186–8; Herring, *America's Longest War*, p. 331.
8. Bui Diem with David Chanoff, *In the Jaws of History* (Boston, MA: Houghton Mifflin, 1987), pp. 341–2.
9. Van Tien Dung, *Our Great Spring Victory* (New York: Monthly Review Press, 1977), p. 125; Military History Institute of Vietnam, *Victory in*

Vietnam: The Official History of the People's Army of Vietnam, 1954–1975, trans. Merle L. Pribbenow (Lawrence: University Press of Kansas, 2002), p. 357.

10. Nguyen Tien Hung and Jerrold L. Schecter, *The Palace File* (New York: Harper & Row, 1986), p. 240.
11. Anderson, 'Gerald R. Ford,' pp. 197–9.
12. Arthur J. Dommen, *The Indochinese Experience of the French and the Americans: Nationalism and Communism in Cambodia, Laos, and Vietnam* (Bloomington: Indiana University Press, 2001), pp. 840, 931–7.
13. Hess, *Vietnam and the United States*, pp. 154–5.
14. Herring, *America's Longest War*, pp. 362–4.
15. Fred A. Wilcox, *Waiting for an Army to Die: The Tragedy of Agent Orange* (New York: Vintage, 1983), pp. 175–81; Lester H. Brune and Richard Dean Burns, *America and the Indochina Wars, 1945–1990: A Bibliographical Guide* (Claremont, CA: Regina Books, 1992), p. 183.
16. David L. Anderson, ed., *Facing My Lai: Moving beyond the Massacre* (Lawrence: University Press of Kansas, 1998), pp. 139–51.
17. Jerold M. Starr, 'Why Study Vietnam?' ibid., pp. 213–21.
18. Herring, *America's Longest War*, p. 357; Robert D. Schulzinger, *A Time for War: The United States and Vietnam, 1941–1975* (New York: Oxford University Press, 1997), p. 329.
19. Gary R. Hess, 'The Unending Debate: Historians and the Vietnam War,' *Diplomatic History* 18 (Spring 1994): 239–64.
20. Ngo Vinh Long quoted in Mark Jason Gilbert, 'The Cost of Losing the "Other War" in Vietnam,' in Marc Jason Gilbert, ed., *How the North Won the Vietnam War* (New York: Palgrave – now Palgrave Macmillan, 2002), p. 187.
21. William J. Duiker, *Sacred War: Nationalism and Revolution in a Divided Vietnam* (New York: McGraw-Hill, 1995), pp. 251–8.
22. George C. Herring, 'Preparing Not to Fight the Last War: The Impact of the Vietnam War on the U.S. Military,' in Charles E. Neu, ed., *After Vietnam: Legacies of a Lost War* (Baltimore, MD: Johns Hopkins University Press, 2000), pp. 73–80.
23. *Public Papers of the Presidents of the United States: George Bush, 1991* (Washington, DC: Government Printing Office, 1992), pp. 196–7.

Selective Bibliography

General histories and reference works

Anderson, David L. *The Columbia Guide to the Vietnam War*. New York Columbia University Press, 2002.

Anderson, David L., ed. *Shadow on the White House: Presidents and the Vietnam War, 1945–1975*. Lawrence: University Press of Kansas, 1993.

DeGroot, Gerard J. *A Noble Cause? America and the Vietnam War*. Harlow: Longman, 2000.

Fitzgerald, Frances. *Fire in the Lake: The Vietnamese and the Americans in Vietnam*. Boston, MA: Little, Brown, 1972.

Herring, George C. *America's Longest War: The United States and Vietnam, 1950–1975*. 4th edn, Boston, MA: McGraw-Hill, 2002.

Hess, Gary R. *Vietnam and the United States: Origins and Legacy of War*. Rev. edn, Boston, MA: Twayne Publishers, 1998.

Karnow, Stanley. *Vietnam: A History*. New York: Viking Press, 1992.

Langguth, A. J. *Our Vietnam: The War, 1954–1975*. New York: Simon and Schuster, 2000.

Lowe, Peter, ed. *The Vietnam War*. Basingstoke: Macmillan – now Palgrave Macmillan, 1998.

Moïse, Edwin E. *Historical Dictionary of the Vietnam War*. Lanham, MD: Rowman and Littlefield, 2002.

Moss, George Donelson. *Vietnam: An American Ordeal*. 4th edn, Upper Saddle River, NJ: Prentice Hall, 2002.

Schulzinger, Robert D. *A Time for War: The United States and Vietnam, 1941–1975*. New York: Oxford University Press, 1997.

Tucker, Spencer. *Vietnam*. Lexington: University Press of Kentucky, 1999.

Tucker, Spencer, ed. *Encyclopedia of the Vietnam War: A Political,*

Social, and Military History. 3 vols, Santa Barbara, CA: ABC-CLIO, 1998.
Young, Marilyn B. *The Vietnam Wars, 1945–1990*. New York: HarperCollins, 1991.

Vietnamese history

Brigham, Robert K. *Guerrilla Diplomacy: The NLF's Foreign Relations and the Viet Nam War*. Ithaca, NY: Cornell University Press, 1999.
Buttinger, Joseph. *Vietnam: A Political History*. New York: Praeger, 1972.
Duiker, William J. *Ho Chi Minh*. New York: Hyperion, 2000.
Duiker, William J. *Sacred War: Nationalism and Revolution in a Divided Vietnam*. New York: McGraw-Hill, 1995.
McAlister, John T., Jr. *Viet Nam: The Origins of Revolution*. New York: Knopf, 1969.
Military History Institute of Vietnam, *Victory in Vietnam: The Official History of the People's Army of Vietnam, 1954–1975*. Trans. Merle L. Pribbenow. Lawrence: University Press of Kansas, 2002.
Pike, Douglas. *History of Vietnamese Communism*. Stanford, CA: Stanford University Press, 1978.
Race, Jeffrey. *War Comes to Long An: Revolutionary Conflict in a Vietnamese Village*. Berkeley: University of California Press, 1972.
Taylor, Keith Weller. *The Birth of Vietnam*. Berkeley: University of California Press, 1983.

French colonialism and the Franco–Vietminh War

Bradley, Mark Philip. *Imagining Vietnam and America: The Making of Postcolonial Vietnam, 1919–1950*. Chapel Hill: University of North Carolina Press, 2000.
Gardner, Lloyd C. *Approaching Vietnam: From World War II through Dienbienphu*. New York: Norton, 1988.
Hammer, Ellen. *The Struggle for Indochina, 1940–1955*. Stanford, CA: Stanford University Press, 1966.
Hess, Gary R. *The United States' Emergence as a Southeast Asian Power, 1940–1950*. New York: Columbia University Press, 1987.
Marr, David G. *Vietnamese Tradition on Trial, 1920–1945*. Berkeley: University of California Press, 1981.

Marr, David G. *Vietnamese Anticolonialism*. Berkeley: University of California Press, 1971.

Ngo Vinh Long. *Before the Revolution: The Vietnamese Peasants Under the French*. New York: Columbia University Press, 1991.

Shaplen, Robert. *The Lost Revolution: The U.S. in Vietnam, 1946–1966*. Rev. edn, New York: Harper and Row, 1966.

Short, Anthony. *The Origins of the Vietnam War*. London: Longman, 1989.

Tønnesson, Stein. *The Vietnamese Revolution of 1945: Roosevelt, Ho Chi Minh, and de Gaulle in a World at War*. Oslo: International Peace Research Institute, 1991.

The United States encounters Vietnam, 1953–1963

Anderson, David L. *Trapped by Success: The Eisenhower Administration and Vietnam, 1953–1961*. New York: Columbia University Press, 1991.

Fall, Bernard B. *The Two Viet-Nams: A Political and Military History*. New York: Praeger. 1967.

Freedman, Lawrence. *Kennedy's Wars: Berlin, Cuba, Laos, and Vietnam*. New York: Oxford University Press, 2000.

Jones, Howard. *Death of a Generation: How the Assassinations of Diem and JFK Prolonged the Vietnam War*. New York: Oxford University Press, 2003.

Kahin, George McT. *Intervention: How America Became Involved in Vietnam*. New York: Knopf, 1986.

Kaiser, David. *American Tragedy: Kennedy, Johnson, and the Origins of the Vietnam War*. Cambridge, MA: Harvard University Press, 2000.

The American war in Vietnam, 1964–1968

Appy, Christian G. *Working-Class War: American Combat Soldiers and Vietnam*. Chapel Hill: University of North Carolina Press, 1993.

Berman, Larry. *Lyndon Johnson's War*. New York: Norton, 1989.

Berman, Larry. *Planning a Tragedy: The Americanization of the War in Vietnam*. New York: Norton, 1982.

DeBenedetti, Charles, and Charles Chatfield. *An American Ordeal: The Antiwar Movement of the Vietnam Era*. Syracuse, NY: Syracuse University Press, 1990.

Frankum, Ronald Bruce. *Like Rolling Thunder: The Air War in Vietnam, 1964–1975*. Lanham, MD: Rowman & Littlefield, 2005.

Gaiduk, Ilya V. *The Soviet Union and the Vietnam War*. Chicago: Ivan R. Dee, 1996.

Gardner, Lloyd C. *Pay Any Price: Lyndon Johnson and the Wars for Vietnam*. Chicago: Ivan R. Dee, 1995.

Halberstam, David. *The Best and the Brightest*. New York: Random House, 1972.

Hammond, William M. *Reporting Vietnam: Media and Military at War*. Lawrence: University Press of Kansas, 1998.

Herring, George C. *LBJ and Vietnam: A Different Kind of War*. Austin: University of Texas Press, 1994.

Johnson, Lyndon. *The Vantage Point: Perspectives of the Presidency, 1963–1969*. New York: Popular Library, 1971.

Logevall, Fredrik. *Choosing War: The Lost Chance for Peace and the Escalation of War in Vietnam*. Berkeley: University of California Press, 1999.

McNamara, Robert S. *In Retrospect: The Tragedy and Lessons of Vietnam*. New York: Times Books, 1995.

Moïse, Edwin E. *Tonkin Gulf and the Escalation of the Vietnam War*. Chapel Hill: University of North Carolina Press, 1996.

Oberdorfer, Don. *Tet!* Garden City, NY: Doubleday, 1977.

Prados, John. *The Blood Road: The Ho Chi Minh Trail and the Vietnam War*. New York: John Wiley, 1999.

Schell, Jonathan. *The Real War: The Classic Reporting on the Vietnam War*. New York: Pantheon, 1987.

Small, Melvin. *Antiwarriors: The Vietnam War and the Battle for America's Hearts and Minds*. Wilmington, DE: Scholarly Resources, 2002.

Summers, Harry G., Jr. *On Strategy: A Critical Analysis of the Vietnam War*. Novato, CA: Presidio Press, 1982.

Wells, Tom. *The War Within: America's Battle Over Vietnam*. Berkeley: University of California Press, 1994.

Zhai Qiang. *China and the Vietnam Wars, 1950–1975*. Chapel Hill: University of North Carolina Press, 2000.

The end of the war, 1969–1975

Berman, Larry. *No Peace, No Honor: Nixon, Kissinger, and Betrayal in Vietnam*. New York: The Free Press, 2001.

Goodman, Allen E. *The Lost Peace: America's Search for a Negotiated Settlement of the Vietnam War*. Stanford, CA: Hoover Institution Press, 1978.

Isaacs, Arnold R. *Without Honor: Defeat in Vietnam and Cambodia*. New York: Vintage Books, 1984.

Kimball, Jeffrey. *The Vietnam War Files: Uncovering the Secret History of Nixon-Era Strategy*. Lawrence: University Press of Kansas, 2004.

Kimball, Jeffrey. *Nixon's Vietnam War*. Lawrence: University Press of Kansas, 1998.

Kissinger, Henry. *Years of Upheaval*. Boston, MA: Little, Brown, 1982.

Kissinger, Henry. *The White House Years*. Boston, MA: Little, Brown, 1979.

Nixon, Richard M. *RN: The Memoirs of Richard Nixon*. New York: Warner Books, 1978.

Sorley, Lewis. *A Better War: The Unexamined Victories and Final Tragedy of America's Last Years in Vietnam*. New York: Harcourt Brace, 1999.

Van Tien Dung. *Our Great Spring Victory: An Account of the Liberation of South Vietnam*. New York: Monthly Review Press, 1977.

Lessons and legacies

Baritz, Loren. *Backfire: A History of How American Culture Led Us Into Vietnam and Made Us Fight the Way We Did*. New York: Morrow, 1985.

Chanda, Nayan. *Brother Enemy: The War After the War*. New York: Harcourt Brace Jovanovich, 1986.

Franklin, H. Bruce. *M.I.A. or Mythmaking in America*. New Bruswick, NJ: Rutgers University Press, 1994.

Gelb, Leslie, and Richard K. Betts. *The Irony of Vietnam: The System Worked*. Washington, DC: Brookings Institution, 1979.

Gilbert, Marc Jason, ed. *How the North Won the Vietnam War*. New York: Palgrave – now Palgrave Macmillan, 2002.

Isaacs, Arnold R. *Vietnam Shadows: The War, Its Ghosts, and Its Legacy*. Baltimore, MD: Johns Hopkins University Press, 1997.

Levy, David W. *The Debate Over Vietnam*. 2nd edn, Baltimore, MD: Johns Hopkins University Press, 1995.

MacPherson, Myra. *Long Time Passing: Vietnam and the Haunted Generation*. Garden City, NY: Doubleday, 1984.

Podhoretz, Norman. *Why We Were in Vietnam*. New York: Simon and Schuster, 1983.

Record, Jeffrey. *The Wrong War: Why We Lost in Vietnam*. Annapolis, MD: Naval Institute Press, 1998.

Index